Ethics
and the Practice of
Forensic Science

INTERNATIONAL FORENSIC SCIENCE AND INVESTIGATION SERIES

Series Editor: Max Houck

INTERNATIONAL FORENSIC SCIENCE
AND INVESTIGATION SERIES

Ethics
and the Practice of
Forensic Science

Robin T. Bowen

CRC Press
Taylor & Francis Group
Boca Raton   London   New York

CRC Press is an imprint of the
Taylor & Francis Group, an **informa** business

CRC Press
Taylor & Francis Group
6000 Broken Sound Parkway NW, Suite 300
Boca Raton, FL 33487-2742

© 2010 by Taylor and Francis Group, LLC
CRC Press is an imprint of Taylor & Francis Group, an Informa business

No claim to original U.S. Government works

Printed in the United States of America on acid-free paper
10 9 8 7 6 5 4 3 2 1

International Standard Book Number: 978-1-4200-8893-9 (Hardback)

Library of Congress Cataloging-in-Publication Data

Bowen, Robin T.
　　Ethics and the practice of forensic science / Robin T. Bowen.
　　　　p. cm. -- (International forensic science and investigation series)
　　Includes bibliographical references and index.
　　ISBN 978-1-4200-8893-9 (hardcover : alk. paper)
　　1. Forensic sciences--Moral and ethical aspects--United States. 2. Forensic scientists--Professional ethics--United States. 3. Forensic sciences--Moral and ethical aspects. 4. Forensic scientists--Professional ethics. I. Title. II. Series.

HV8073.B649 2010
174'.936325--dc22
　　2009042280

Visit the Taylor & Francis Web site at
http://www.taylorandfrancis.com

and the CRC Press Web site at
http://www.crcpress.com

This book is dedicated to all the professionals
struggling to find the right answer...

And to my husband, for always helping me to find my right answers.

Table of Contents

Foreword

DOUGLAS M. LUCAS

Forensic scientists have been assisting the judicial process throughout the world for at least several hundred years through the provision of scientific and technical information derived from physical evidence of all kinds. This information has been, and continues to be, delivered in the form of verbal or written reports to investigators and attorneys or by means of *viva voce* testimony in courts or tribunals of various kinds. Throughout this time, these specialized scientists and technicians have usually performed their examinations according to the appropriate professional standards of the day and the generally accepted ethics of their professions. In earlier times, the latter were generally intuitive rather than promulgated, but in more recent years professional codes of ethics have been developed to assist in the guidance of what is and is not acceptable.

Notwithstanding this, the timing of the publication of this book on ethical practices in forensic science could not have been more appropriate. The interest of the general public in ethical performance in all fields has been stimulated by the well-publicized departures from ethical practice by some business executives (at, e.g., Enron, AIG, Martha Stewart Omnimedia) and by some in the world of sports (e.g., figure skating judges at the Salt Lake City Olympics, performance-enhancing drug users). Such deviations from acceptable practice have not been restricted to boardrooms or athletic venues; sadly, some have also occurred in forensic science laboratories. Although the numbers are relatively small, such events, when they do occur, develop very high profiles. Major media headlines have been generated by issues in, for example, the laboratories of the Federal Bureau of Investigation (FBI), the Detroit Police Department, and the Houston Police Department. The latter resulted in more than 200 articles in a single newspaper over a four-year period.

The enhanced interest of the public at large in ethics has been mirrored by additional emphasis by the forensic science profession on ethical conduct. In 2008, the principal forensic science laboratory accrediting body, the American Society of Crime Laboratory Directors Laboratory Accreditation Board (ASCLD/LAB), began to require that staff of accredited labs receive training in the application of ethical practices in forensic science.

In February 2009, the U.S. National Academy of Sciences in its report *Strengthening Forensic Science in the United States: A Path Forward* recommended the following:

The National Institute of Forensic Science (NIFS), in consultation with its advisory board, should establish a national code of ethics for all forensic science disciplines and encourage individual societies to incorporate this national code as part of their professional code of ethics. Additionally, NIFS should explore mechanisms of enforcement for those forensic scientists who commit serious ethical violations. Such a code could be enforced through a certification process for forensic scientists. (Recommendation 9)

Many of the forensic science organizations in North America have, in fact, had ethics codes for 30 years or more; the first Code of Ethics of the American Academy of Forensic Sciences, for example, was approved by its membership in 1976.

While codes of ethics of different professional organizations may vary widely in their format, they all have (or should have) one thing in common: They should represent a distillation of a profession's collected historical experience and wisdom. Their provisions can thus be readily accepted by the members of the profession and become the rules by which the profession operates. They can offer guidance and support about a course of action in a particular situation although they may not provide unambiguous answers to specific questions.

Training in ethics begins long before professional activity is even contemplated; the mentors are parents, teachers, and spiritual advisors. Training occurs largely through a form of osmosis. Professional ethical concepts can then be added to supplement the base foundation, but it is not an exaggeration to state that in the absence of a well-developed sense of personal morality an unequivocal acceptance of ethical responsibility is unattainable.

Teaching ethics is therefore extremely difficult, if not impossible, and this book makes clear that its purpose is not so much to teach ethics as it is to create for the reader an awareness of the subject and to provide a greater appreciation of the professional culture of forensic science. It discusses concepts in the abstract and then tries to assist by asking questions with specific contexts. Some situations, such as misrepresentation of credentials, are very straightforward, but others such as competence and whistle-blowing can produce situational dilemmas. Not all situations are black or white with good or bad answers. Many are gray with only good and better or bad and worse solutions. This book assists readers in dealing with ethical challenges by providing crutches to help them walk but not a motorized wheelchair to carry them through a sometimes muddy field.

Preface

What is ethics? How do ethics differ from morals? What ethical concerns are inherent to forensic science? Everyone learns basic ethics from the time he or she is born, so why is it necessary to explore the topic? Who decides what is ethical? These are just some of the questions posed when discussing the topic of ethics in regard to forensic scientists. Approaching the topic of ethics is quite daunting for a variety of reasons: It is philosophical in nature, there is not always a clear distinction between right and wrong, and it is closely related to religion. Personal character may influence ethical decisions, and to fully explore the subject people should possess open-mindedness and a willingness to discuss their points of view. Answers to these questions and many more will be presented in a manner that encourages contemplation, discussion, and reflection. The reader should consider the information provided and relate this to his or her everyday life.

Forensic science is a profession of scientists whose work answers questions for the law through reports and testimony (Houck and Siegel, 2006). It is composed of a variety of disciplines that work with the legal system. Common statements made to me by the general forensic community in regard to ethics include the following:

- Forensic scientists are ethical by nature.
- It is not possible to teach a person ethics; either he or she is ethical or not.
- The topic of ethics is boring and too philosophical.
- A course, lecture, or text is not going to make an unethical person ethical.
- Just explain what is right and wrong for given situations so ethical dilemmas are not an issue.

Although such points have some validity, they do not provide a clear picture of the purpose in discussing ethics as it relates to forensic science.

Though everyone would like to believe that all forensic scientists are ethical in nature, it is simply not the case. Circumstances coupled with pressure, motivation, and opportunity can cause anyone to cross the proverbial ethical line. Throughout my years of studying ethics as it relates to forensic science, the statement, "You cannot teach someone ethics," has been a recurring theme. The point of publications that explore the topic of ethics is not necessarily to *teach* ethics as much as to create *awareness* of the subject. Knowledge, discussion, and thought are important to prevent ethical dilemmas. Information also provides people with the tools necessary to refocus after misconduct affects the workplace or the profession. Finally, although it would be much easier to have a rulebook containing dos and don'ts for every situation professionals may encounter, it is unrealistic. Variables, such as the people involved, the agencies and their affiliations, the circumstances of the situations, and the consequences and effect on innocent people, create unique situations. Due to these variables, it is impossible to have a set of rules that comprise any and all situations.

Ethics is an extremely important topic in professional cultures such as law, business, medicine, science, and technology. A *culture* is a large group of people with shared beliefs, laws, morals, standards, and characteristics. This common view influences behavior, communication methods, and values. *Values* describe a belief that a specific method of conduct is personally or socially preferred. Components of professional cultures include managerial styles, traditions, loyalties, hierarchy, and decision-making rules. It is important to explore how cultures communicate with and about each other to gain a deeper understanding. Discussing ethics among cultures begins with recognizing common interests or goals and valuing diversity. To work with other cultures, it is imperative to understand their values, to maintain positive cooperation and conflict resolution, to determine potential diversity within the culture, to listen carefully, and to show respect for differences. Most professions have had examples of misconduct. Throughout this book we will explore the intricacies of ethics as it relates to the forensic science profession. By the end of this book, the reader will have a greater appreciation of the professional culture of forensic science as well as the professional cultures that work with and against the rules of the forensic science profession.

What are your beliefs? How do you put them into practice in your career?

Series Editor

Max M. Houck is director of the Forensic Science Initiative, a program that develops research and professional training for forensic scientists and related professionals. Houck is a trace evidence expert and forensic anthropologist. Houck is also director of forensic business development in the College of Business and Economics at West Virginia University (WVU). He was chair of the Forensic Science Educational Program Accreditation Commission (FEPAC) from 2004 to 2008. Houck has authored or co-authored four books and an introductory forensic science textbook, *Fundamentals of Forensic Science,* was co-authored with Dr. Jay Siegel. Houck serves on the editorial boards of the *Journal of Forensic Sciences* and the *Journal of Forensic Identification.* Houck has appeared on *Forensic Files, The New Detectives, National Geographic,* and *E! Entertainment.*

Acknowledgments

The journey of writing this book began with the desire to fill a void in the forensic community. Science is ever changing, and through the years since my research began, ethics has become quite a hot topic. Although people recognize that ethics and forensic science are inseparable (or at least *should* be), I am told time and time again that it is impossible to teach a person to be ethical. I hope that in reading this book you discover, as so many forensic practitioners have, that "learning about ethics" is about awareness, questioning, and consideration of the pressures placed on forensic scientists. I would like to express my gratitude to all of the people who conveyed the need for ethics training as well as to all of those who told me that it was not necessary. The scientists who have unknowingly gone down the wrong path and those of you who were grateful for the information I collected were the inspiration for this book, and I am grateful.

I am lucky to be surrounded by such a wonderful support system of family, friends, and colleagues. First, I would like to thank the Forensic Science Initiative office for putting up with my ethical "picking" and for always teaching me something. I would like to thank all of the friends who supported me and sacrificed time for this book—it is wonderful to know that you are in my life and do not hold grudges for my lengthy hiatuses! I would like to thank my families and especially my parents, Arlene and Bernie Stoehr and Leanne and Jim Bowen, for the sheer joy on your faces as you found out that I had writing a book up my sleeve (and for allowing me to miss the occasional holiday to do so). I would like to thank Liz Richardson and Samantha Neal for taking the time to make comments on drafts of this book and Brandon Smithson for his creativity and enthusiasm to design the cover. I would like to thank my wonderful husband, Matt, and my mascot ("ethics dog") for the patience, support, and entertaining time-outs they provided. Finally I would like to thank Max, my friend and mentor, who nudges me into new opportunities and experiences—and then guides me through the journey. I appreciate each and every person who has supported me along the way and made this book possible.

Author

Robin Bowen is assistant director for the Forensic Science Initiative, a program that develops research, scientific resources, and professional training and continuing education for forensic scientists and related professionals. Her primary responsibilities include coordination of continuing education programs, management of research projects, and correspondence of progress to the National Institute of Justice. Bowen is the primary developer of the Forensic Educational Alliance, an initiative to offer a variety of forensic science continuing education courses online. She has an undergraduate degree in forensic and investigative sciences and a graduate degree in secondary science education. Bowen is a member of the American Academy of Forensic Science, International Association for Identification, and National Science Teachers Association. Over the last four years, ethics as it relates to forensic science has been her primary research topic and has culminated in a successful Web-based continuing education course as well as workshops provided to the forensic community.

What Is Ethics?

1

Introduction

Ethics is a branch of philosophy dealing with what is morally right and wrong, good and bad. *Right* and *wrong* refers to behaviors or conduct, while *good* and *bad* refers to outcomes and consequences of behaviors. The discussion of ethics in forensic science explores a profession that shares moral values or qualities within its own community and in relation to coexisting professions. Ethics can be viewed as the general study of the ideals regarding human behavior and the guiding principles. People typically think of ethics as practical knowledge, not theoretical knowledge; in reality, it is both. Ethics are not meant to dictate actions but to offer the tools and direction for dealing with situations. The goal of ethics is to protect the rights and needs of professions (or groups) when situations are not just "black and white." Ethics are standards of conduct that *prescribe* behavior but do not *describe* actual behavior. If ethics deal with right and wrong in terms of ideals, then what constitutes morals, and how do these differ from ethics?

Morality is the "operational side" of ethics that provides a basis of right and wrong for ethical application. Ethics are applicable to situations and are "practiced" while morals are "known." Morals tend to be specific and generally agreed on standards of conduct in society. Though people tend to confuse *ethics* and *morals*, morality and integrity are more similar and may be used interchangeably when referring to actions. Honesty and integrity are society's *most* general values that apply to everyone (right or wrong). Just because people are honest and have morals does not mean that they will not face ethical issues at some point in their lives. Learning about ethics as it relates to a profession will serve as a guide to overcome ethical dilemmas. The learning process involves constant questioning and discussion of ethical values. Ethical principles, such as obligation, fairness, mercy, and duty, are validated by consistency, relevant factors, and suitability for human experience.

Moral standards may be universal even if moral judgment is influenced by society. Aristotle's virtue theory's perspective is that the goal of ethics is the development of moral goodness. A person must portray character traits that fit social and moral values while having the desire to act morally. A person who seeks to make practical moral judgments will strive for moderation in lieu of extremes. Although moderation depends on the individual, appropriate actions are dictated through reason. According to Socrates, "Virtue is knowledge and knowledge is virtue." In other words, if a person knows what is right, he or she will act on what is right. This statement also implies that wrongdoing is involuntary and based on unawareness, which illustrates the reason for some examples of unethical behavior that we examine in upcoming chapters. So how does a person know what actions are right? A study conducted by James Rest and his colleagues determined that ethical behavior is a result of four processes: (1) *moral sensitivity* or the ability to interpret situations, recognize the ethical issue, and understand consequences; (2) *moral judgment* or the ability to decide which act is morally justified; (3) *moral motivation* or the commitment to doing what is ethical, using ethical standards, and taking responsibility for consequences; and (4) *moral character* or the courage, determination, and confidence to execute ethical behavior (Johannesen 2008). Before moving forward, we must first take a look at the evolution of ethics as a branch of philosophy and the various schools of thought on the topic.

Ethical Theories

Ethics is the analysis of fundamental moral concepts of right and wrong. Ethical theories guide people through moral problem solving. Theories are hypotheses that explain a topic or problem and are evaluated based on their rationality, consistency, and usefulness to the issue in question. Ethical theories should be general, supportive, abstract, noncontradicting, internally consistent, and in agreement with moral intuition. The main features of ethical theories reduce difficulty of problems by providing general principles that are relative to a variety of issues, provide a checks and balances system for moral principles based on consistency, and expand areas of knowledge (in regards to other disciplines).

The subject of ethics is subdivided into the following theories: normative ethics, metaethics, and applied ethics. Normative ethics is the study of moral standards, principles, concepts, values, and theories and seeks to determine what is right or wrong to justify standards for behavior. This type of theory is the foundation for creating moral principles of conduct for decision making. Metaethics is the study of the nature of moral standards, principles, values, and theories. Metaethics explores the meanings of moral concepts and analyzes the moral reasoning. Applied ethics is the study of ethical dilemmas, choices, and standards of application in particular contexts including occupations, professions, and situations. Applied ethics are investigations of moral conduct based on facts and are the focus when discussing the ethics of forensic science.

The Study of Ethics

Some important steps should be taken when studying ethics. The first step encourages awareness and receptiveness to moral and ethical issues. The second step supports the development of critical thinking and analytical skills. During the second step, one learns to better distinguish concepts and to prevent "bad" solutions. A bad solution may cause more problems if the right questions are not asked from the beginning. An example of a bad solution might be, "Isabelle forgot to sign the evidence log. I know she was the last examiner to have the evidence, so I will just sign her name since she probably forgot." This example shows a bad solution that began with good intentions. The solution, although good for the present time, could create more problems in the future. In this example, additional problems will occur when the original examiner is questioned regarding the evidence log in court. The critical thinking step provides the necessary skills for people to learn how to convey information to colleagues or supervisors to assure that the proper procedures are taken to correct current and future mistakes. The third step in studying ethics occurs when people become more personally responsible. Using the first two steps and increasing the ability to respond to situations will help people achieve personal responsibility. Gaining a sense of personal responsibility will create a sense of empowerment for people and will lead to more productive searches for truth. The final step is to recognize how professional cultures operate. In this case, forensic science as a profession seeks to use scientific evidence to provide information related to crimes. In striving to meet the goal of the profession, the trust given to forensic scientists may create the potential for corruption and abuse of power. As Doug Lucas (2007) states, *"We are holders of a public trust because a portion of the vital affairs of other people has been placed into our hands by virtue of the role of our laboratories in the criminal justice system."* To assure ethical behavior, the professionals in the field must undergo a checks and balances system. Cumulatively, the steps taken when studying ethics are applied in a certain context.

To understand ethics, it is important to have an awareness of the varying contexts in which ethics is studied. The first, *personal context,* is the objective testing and questioning of personal values and ethics. It is a person's individual sense of ethics and justice. There are five elements to personal ethics: (1) discretion, or the ability to make choices in situations that have no clear rules; (2) duty, or deciding between competing obligations; (3) honesty; (4) loyalty; and (5) respect for others. People may also study ethics in a *social context.* The social context involves how people relate to others based on the given circumstances. In this context, understanding a person's history and environment before judging his or her actions is essential. *Criminal justice* is a process-specific context used to study ethics as it relates to law and enforcement procedures. This context combines aspects of social and personal perspectives to deliberate new laws. Criminal justice must balance peace and order, liberty and security, and fulfillment and happiness to adequately merge social and personal contexts. *If something is illegal, does it mean that it is ethical?* The law is what people *must* do, while ethics are what people *should* do. Some examples of laws that are unethical include slavery, prohibition, religious rules concerning customary dress, and minority citizens' right to vote. Another example is protestors of the Vietnam War; though illegal, the people felt that their actions were justified ethically. Forensic ethics is studied by understanding personal, social, and criminal justice contexts. Once contexts of ethics are better understood, approaches to ethical theories may be explored.

Utilitarianism: The Greater Good

The utilitarian approach is also known as the consequentialist or teleological ethical theory. The basic principle is that human beings judge morality of actions in terms of the consequences or results of those actions. Moral acts elicit good consequences—those that create happiness and are justifiable. Immoral acts elicit bad consequences—those that induce pain and suffering and are unjustifiable. In this approach actions may be moral or immoral based on the capacity to achieve the greatest good for the greatest number of people. For example, an increase in funding for crime laboratories is good because it helps the agencies, the employees, and society. In contrast, an increase in funding specifically for a single discipline within the laboratory would not impact as many people. In this case, then, the former is considered the moral act.

John Stuart Mill (1806–1873) and Jeremy Bentham (1748–1832) developed the utilitarian outcome-based approach in the 18th and 19th centuries. Bentham focused on the concept of pleasure versus pain, while Mill studied happiness versus unhappiness. Although Mill contributed to developing the approach, he disagreed with Bentham as he was more concerned with the quality of happiness rather than the quantity. Pleasure and pain are determined by considering the duration, intensity, long-term consequences, and likelihood of outcomes to all parties influenced by the action. Summing up all consequences and assessing the outcome assure that individual interests are considered.

Bentham used normative ethics by seeking which behavior is morally right or wrong and trying to establish norms for behavior. His goal was to merge competing views: the nature of man's ego with societal influence and goals. He felt that man and society could coexist based on common motivations he referred to as *sanctions*: (1) physical sanctions, or the natural sensation of happiness and pain; (2) political sanctions, the legal acts that can counteract immoral acts; (3) moral sanctions, approval or disapproval from those around a person; and (4) religious sanctions, the blessing or condemning by a supreme being, consistent with one's faith. The weakness of his theory was that the core principle was vague and did not account for individual rights. The principle evolved and became known as the *greatest happiness principle,* which allowed more needs to be met within a community. The new version of the principle focuses on the morality of an action that creates happiness or the principle of utility.

Belief in hedonism was the basis for Bentham's work, as it was the most famous version of the utilitarian theory where the fundamental good is happiness. Whichever action produces the greatest amount of happiness for the most people is considered the most moral act. Although this seems straightforward, many problems make the concept of *happiness* hard to employ. First, the greatest happiness is achieved at the expense of the fewest people. Consider this: It is not always possible to predict consequences for everyone involved. While we do make decisions based on consequences, this philosophy may lead to situations with no set of rules or standards. Finally, happiness could appear to condone some actions with which most people would not agree, such as a person gaining happiness through child pornography, creating potential conflicts with individual human rights.

The three primary criticisms of utilitarianism are listed here and are followed by the utilitarian response to the statement. First, what gives people the ability to weigh unlike things and to rate one's own happiness against others? Utilitarians counter by stating that conscience should serve as a guide. Next, utilitarianism does not differentiate between obligatory acts (actions that are wrong to omit) and supererogatory acts (morally good actions, but beyond necessary moral obligation). Utilitarians believe that because one's happiness is accounted for, supererogatory acts are not required. Finally, one must put individual goals aside to first meet the goals of the greater good. Utilitarians state that people need to give up personal goals only if those goals conflict with morality. So how do we alleviate these problems?

Cases of conflicting duties require that action be taken in a situation if and only if (1) doing the action (a) treats as few people as possible as mere means to an end; and (b) treats as many people as ends as consistent with treating as few people as possible as mere means to the ends; and (2) taking the action in the situation brings about as much overall happiness as consistent with actually doing the action. These guidelines, presented in *Justice, Crime, and Ethics,* will assist a person in circumventing problems of binding and conflicting duties. They will also focus attention onto what is specifically good or bad for the greatest amount of people. The whole process has been described as *systemized common sense.*

Deontological Ethics: Obligation and Intention

Immanuel Kant, an 18th-century German philosopher, believed that humans have certain duties regardless of the consequences they evoke. The deontological approach states that moral actions occur out of obligation and are judged based on the intention and motivation for the action. Duty is an expression of free will to do the right thing even if no one is paying attention. If a person performs his or her duty, the action is considered right because duties are morally binding obligations. Actions not motivated by duty are motivated by inclination, self-interest, or impulse. There are two primary levels of deontological theories. The first level is "extreme" or "inconsequential," in which consequences are not considered at all; people believe that consequences have no relationship to morals. An example of this view is a person's duty to tell the truth, no matter the potential consequences. A forensic scientist should state the facts and opinions regarding evidence even if the facts provide support for the opposing counsel's case. Another common duty is the duty to help others. According to the extreme deontological theory, helping others is good even if the person is helping to do something wrong. For example, as a fellow crime scene investigator is swabbing bloodstain evidence he or she contaminates the sample. In the spirit of deontological theory, the person's coworker helps the investigator by omitting that particular swab from the evidence log. Although this is helpful to the investigator, it is noncompliant with proper procedure. The duty of helping is fulfilled without regard to the consequences.

The second level of deontological theory is "moderate," in which consequences are applied in addition to other factors; this level is much closer to consequentialist theory. Kant believed that the consequentialists, those who follow the Utilitarian approach, are omitting a large part of ethics by neglecting their duty and the intention to do right. Kant demonstrated his feeling by stating, "It is impossible to conceive anything at all in the world, or even out of it, which can be taken as good without qualification, except *good will*" (Kant 1964, p. 61). The key to the deontological approach is human intention rather than consequences of given actions (e.g., "I *intended* to sign the chain of custody form before handing it over to the chemistry section"). Moral worth is based on the intention of the action; if the action taken is for the sake of duty, it is considered moral under the deontological approach. Suppose a robbery at a local store is called in at the end of a shift; Jim offers to respond to the scene because he knows this will give him overtime pay, while Bernie offers to respond to the scene because he is familiar with the store's owners and wants to help. Although both actions have the same consequence—the scene is staffed and processed—Kant would argue that there is a moral difference. Bernie acted out of his sense of duty, while Jim was motivated by self-interest. Although neither person did anything wrong, one did not have the right motivation, which makes the act immoral according to Kant. Although consequences may be considered in the deontological theory, they are not as important as intention.

One of the main differences between the deontological approach and other ethical models is that a person's ideas do not change from one situation to another. While holding onto ideas eliminates some of the "gray area" that ethical issues often bring, the former relies on all people applying the same reasoning to all situations. Gray areas occur when there is more than one right answer or method and people must choose what is *most* right or *most* wrong in that particular situation. Kant was labeled ignorant, and his approach was highly criticized because of its vast difference from utilitarian views. Kant rejected happiness as a reward for good moral behavior because he felt that happiness is an ideal and cannot be fully comprehended. An example to demonstrate this perspective is drug dealers. The dealers typically have wealth and live in luxury, which one would presume leads them to happiness. If happiness is a virtue, would the drug dealers be considered virtuous despite their method of achieving happiness? According to Kant, instead of thinking, "Will an action make me happy?" the thought is, "Will the action make me *worthy* of happiness?" (Souryal 2003).

The deontological theory is not problem-free. The first problem that may arise is conflicting duties. A duty is anything a human must do; police officers have a duty to arrest people who drive under the influence; forensic scientists have a duty to state what evidence shows; judges have a duty to qualify a subject-matter expert as an expert witness. In all of these duties, the end result may not produce the greatest good or the most happiness; however, the duties are required. What if the duties conflict? For example, if a scientist knows that certain tests need to be completed, it is his or her duty to do so. What if the scientist's supervisor states that the results are needed within the hour? Although the scientist has a duty to complete all necessary testing, he or she also has a duty to obey the supervisor. Which duty is more important and will provide the greatest moral worth? Unfortunately, Kant does not provide guidance as to how duties rank. Another problem with this approach occurs when people begin to make exceptions regarding their own duties. To avoid this issue it is essential to keep in mind that people, as individuals, are no different or more important than anyone else. People must respect the lives of others as much as their own, through fairness and equality, to truly use the deontological approach for an ethical life.

How often do you think this approach occurs in the real world? Do you think that people value others as much as themselves? Do you think it makes a difference if the people are strangers or familiar persons? Do you think the deontological approach is more or less prevalent in forensic science?

Moral actions are guided by duty and are based on "dutiful principles" or laws. The rules of conduct or laws to which Kant refers are *maxims*, such as "honesty is the best policy" or "innocent until proven guilty." Maxims should be universally accepted and commanding so people cannot make up rules as they go and so everyone will act the same way without exception. There are two types of maxims: hypothetical and categorical. Hypothetical maxims are conditional instructions that stress what ought to be done, such as, "If I want to get a job in forensic science, then I *ought* to stay out of trouble." Categorical maxims are unconditional orders to state principles that need to be done, for example, "Tell the truth." In comparison, the hypothetical maxim would state, "If you want to stay out of trouble, tell the truth." In the study of ethics, categorical maxims provide a foundation for ethical decision making.

Kant developed the *categorical imperative,* which is a fundamental principle that allows people to act consistently from situation to situation. The categorical imperative is divided into two formulations. The first formulation is *universalizability,* which states that a justifiable action is when another person faces the same circumstances and acts in the same way. If a person makes a decision that he or she feels is morally justifiable, he or she knows 99 of 100 people would made the same decision. The idea of universalizability may also be described as a person treating everyone the same way as he or she would want to be treated. For example:

> Would I want scientists to retest my evidence if I was in jail and there was a chance that I was innocent? What if I felt that there was a chance the evidence could exonerate me? How does my opinion on this topic change if we are referring to someone else who wants his or her evidence retested?

The second formulation states that people's fundamental value is based on respect for all others and the ability to maintain human dignity. Braswell and McCarthy (2008) stated that one should act in such a way that humanity is treated never simply as a means but also as an end. The categorical imperative principle instructs comprehensively in most all situations.

Comparing Approaches for Forensic Science

The comparison of the utilitarian and the deontological approaches of ethics as they relate to forensic science is better understood when observing a common topic in the field. Take, for example, the opening of cases by the Innocence Project.* In the consequentialist perspective, what are the consequences of

---

* The Innocence Project assists prisoners who have the potential to be proven innocent by DNA testing. The group began its work in 1992 by Barry C. Scheck and Peter J. Neufield. More information can be found at www.innocenceproject.org.

reopening of past cases? Does this act benefit the Innocence Project, society, or both? Is the Innocence Project using society as a means to an end? In examining the consequences, it is helpful to consider outcomes. The potential positive outcomes are freeing individuals who were wrongly convicted, supporting guilt, showing the strength of forensic evidence such as DNA, and giving hope to those who believe they were wrongly convicted. The potential negative outcomes of the Innocence Project include not having the necessary scientists or funding to examine current cases, to complete backlog cases, and to rework past cases. Initially, such pressures may reflect badly on science if people are proven innocent on reexamination of evidence, and more people will want cases reopened or evidence retested, which will take a good deal of time, money, and resources. In the deontologist's view, do those heading the Innocence Project have a duty to reopen past cases? How many cases would scientists be required to retest? Is the Innocence Project serving society by showing potential flaws in science and the judicial system? Based on duty, what legitimate restraints should society impose on the Innocence Project cases?

When considering means–end relationships with either approach, it is useful to answer questions that assist in determining the degree of ethical issues involved. As paraphrased from *Ethics in Human Communication* (Johannesen, Valde, and Whedbee 2008), here are some questions to determine the level of ethics in any means–end relationship:

1. Are the means actually unethical or just unpopular, unwise, or ineffective?
2. Is the end truly good, or does it simply seem so because we want it?
3. Is it possible that the ethically bad means will actually produce a good end?
4. Is the same end achievable using more ethical means?
5. Is the "good" end much better than the potential bad effects of the means used to attain it?
6. Could the use of unethical means be justified to those most affected by them?

Means–end relationships are a crucial factor to consider in ethical decision making.

Ethical Decision Making

Given the information presented, how does one then translate ethical theories and approaches to real-world application? How does a person interpret this knowledge into something useful for personal and professional life? These pieces are part of the bigger picture in that all of the previous information guides ethical decision making. To make ethical decisions it is important to ask the right questions, to focus on the main issues, to balance determination with compromise, to debate possibilities, and to make the decision that stems from the recommended steps. Additional factors that influence ethical decision making include families, friends, environments, community, culture, law, and religion. These factors along with personal opinion shape a person's concept of right and wrong. Cumulatively, the ideas of the various approaches presented provide a foundation to explore the issues involved in ethical decision making.

When attempting to make a decision, analyzing the issue is the best place to begin. The next step is to consider the facts involved: What is beneficial and what is unnecessary? It is then helpful to consider perspectives that others might take regarding the issue. If time allows, open the issue or decision up for debate; asking questions and receiving feedback may help a person discover creative solutions or enable alternate perspectives to emerge. Though feedback is generally positive, it has been shown that social interests tend to have the most significant impact on ethical decision making, stemming from the external pressures. It is not uncommon for decisions to be acquired without adequate time to stop, think, examine, and deliberate the actions for that ethical value. In these cases, people should rely on their personal character as a guide. After the initial process, one or more decisions may emerge. At this point, it is wise to weigh the pros and the cons of each potential outcome: What are the values of the action compared with the consequences that may occur? Applying situational ethics may help a person to rationalize decisions or actions. Situational ethics simply depend on the particular situation's circumstances. However, situational ethics creates a double standard in relation to ethical principles because what works for one person or group may not work for another. These steps provide the initial foundation for ethical decision making.

Typically, moral judgments made in routine situations are easier because there is consistency of choices based on rules and regulations. Unusual situations are more difficult because they can involve conflicting values of religion, culture, or law and are not as familiar to a person. One framework for ethical decision making presented in *Ethics of Human Communication* (Johannesen et al. 2008) stems from Rushworth Kidder regarding ethics in journalism. This framework was developed to explore the underlying structure of decision making:

1. It is an ethical issue and it consists of *x, y,* and *z.*
2. This person/these people are responsible for making the decision.
3. The relevant facts are *x, y,* and *z.*
4. It is truly a matter of right or wrong, ethical or unethical.
5. Is it a choice between competing ethical or "right" actions?
6. Common theories should be applied to determine what is at stake.

7. Look at both options to see if a third option, or compromise, transpires.
8. Make a decision.
9. Evaluate the situation to learn what would or would not be done if the situation occurred again.

Using such frameworks is useful in organizing moral thinking. The four levels of moral thinking that occur are (1) *ideal decision making*, or what is absolutely right or wrong; (2) *practical decision making*, or following common rules such as, "Do not tell lies"; (3) *reflective decision making*, or the exceptions to given rules; and (4) *political decision making*, or making decisions for the good of the larger community (Johannesen et al. 2008).* Ethical judgment is a product of freely made choices, and although the process may result in more questions than answers, the implementation of these organizational strategies can make the process much more manageable. How do people make choices?

Existentialism is a 20th-century concept that focuses on an individual's freedom to make choices without the influence of others. When discussing free will, supporting concepts to consider are *determinism* and *intentionalism*. Determinism means that all thoughts and actions are beyond human control. It can cast doubt on the validity of human choice and manifest itself in a person's attitude, such as, "I was destined to fail" or, "The outcome is fate." Scientific determinism, more specifically, deals with a person's character, conduct, and choices as products of genetics or surroundings. This concept is supported by the following operative elements:

- Genes and chromosomes cause genetic conditions and physiological makeup.
- Climate and geography influence personality and disposition.
- Society and culture provides traditions, beliefs, and tendencies for actions.
- Education and solicitation provide a knowledge base.

Intentionalism is the opposite of determinism in that it maintains that people possess free will and are accountable for their actions. The arguments for intentionalism are as follows:

1. External forces are *influences*, not determinants. Awareness of their effect on decision making decreases their power. People should rationally accept, reject, or alter available options.

---

* Johannesen, R., K. Valde, and K. Whedbee. 2008. *Ethics in Human Communication* (6th Edition). Long Grove, IL: Waveland Press, Inc.

2. People are able to use logical reasoning to make good choices. It is thought that determinists focus too narrowly on cause and effect, thus assuming that preceding events cause the actions that follow.
3. Arguments for determinism are contradictory; the belief is that everything is predetermined, yet they have created the concept of determinism.

The concepts for decision making may seem like unnecessary information, but when examining how decisions are made it becomes clear that such themes are common. People tend to favor the concepts, though they may not realize that the classifications exist. Based on these concepts, is persuasion considered unethical? In the scientific determinism view, surroundings influence decisions, so the answer is likely, "Yes, persuasion is unethical because it can manipulate a person's decision." In the intentionalism view, people make their own choices regardless of external factors, so the answer is likely, "No, persuasion is not unethical because people are accountable for their decisions." What do you think? Is persuasion unethical? What factors could make the influences more or less ethical?

Personal success in the process of ethical decision making requires people to remain honest, compassionate, truthful, and fair. Open-mindedness and sensitivity to alternate perspectives is encouraged because, although achieving happiness is ideal, sacrifice may be necessary to do the "right" thing. Emotion is not a good indicator for ethical decisions because sometimes what is right does not feel good or make us happy. Actions a person should take during the decision-making process include selecting and presenting facts and opinions fairly, favoring public motive over personal cause, and accepting diverse opinions and arguments when presented rationally. In addition, there are qualities that not only will help a person achieve successful decisions but also will expand on his or her existing knowledge and decision-forming methods. Examples of qualities are becoming more aware and open to the broad range of ethical issues (may span from a little white lie to perjury), developing critical thinking and analytical skills (less "how" and more "why"), developing a broad perspective which includes intuition and critical thinking, and becoming more personally responsible. The traits and skills listed contribute to a person's success in ethical decision making.

Framework for Ethical Decisions

Moral questions rarely have clear answers, which is why ethics is a difficult topic to discuss. People tend to get frustrated when things are not black and white; however, think about how often such straightforward situations actually do occur in the real world. For example, do you tell little white lies? Can these lies be justified? Should a person tell a lie if it could save someone's life? What if such a lie was considered justifiable but could put someone else in danger? As mentioned, there are usually more questions than answers in ethical decision making. Though there are various guidelines for conduct, people can rely on some basic formulas or rules for the majority of ethical decisions. The guiding formula for moral judgment as presented consists of the following steps:

- First, select the moral principle that best defines the problem in question; is it a matter of honesty, fairness, equity, or loyalty?
- Second, justify the situation by examining whether it conforms to the selected principle. If not, what accentuating or mitigating factors could make it more or less fitting with the principle?
- Next, if the situation fits the principle exactly, the judgment should be made in exact accordance with the principle.
- Finally, if the situation does not fit the principle exactly, judgment should be made by determining a high or low likelihood that the situation fits the principle. Accentuating factors support a high likelihood and mitigating factors support a low likelihood that the situation will fit the principle.

The formula is not meant to be quantitative; however, it is a useful guide for better moral judgments (Souryal 2003). Many ethical questions are difficult to answer, especially if a person has a biased perspective. In an attempt to lessen bias and to fairly resolve moral judgment, the following rules have been suggested.

Rule 1: Inherent Good Surpasses Noninherent Good

The two categories of goodness are separated by value. Inherent (or intrinsic) goods are valuable objects, actions, or qualities, such as life, liberty, justice, and happiness. Noninherent goods are objects, actions, or qualities whose value depends on the ability to bring about intrinsic good, such as money and loyalty. The overall value is based on resulting accomplishments as opposed to natural value.

For example, which action is right in a given situation, loyalty or honesty? In this case, honesty is the inherent good, so it is the correct choice. Although loyalty may lead to honesty, it in and of itself is a noninherent good, so it should not come before honesty.

Inherent good > noninherent good

Rule 2: Noninherent Evil Surpasses Inherent Evil

This rule is based on the idea that noninherent evil serves as a means for bringing about or maintaining harm (evil) but by itself is not directly harmful. Examples of noninherent evil may include weapons or government; when used properly, no harm is caused. Inherent harm (evil) includes objects, actions, or qualities that are directly harmful, such as death, slavery, or injustice. The goal of this rule is to minimize harmful outcomes.

Noninherent evil > inherent evil

Rule 3: When Selecting between Levels of Good or Evil, Select the Highest Good or the Lowest Evil

The principle of *summum bonum* is a common theme in the study of ethics. It is a principle that examines the hierarchy of choices. Ethical decision making prescribes that a person should strive for the greatest good, or the lowest harm. Many times, ethical decisions are not a matter of right versus wrong; typically they are a matter of what option is *more* right or *more* wrong.

Murder is a good example to demonstrate this concept. Murder could occur in a number of ways including accidental, hanging, lethal injection, poison, or by shooting. Of these options, which is the least harmful? Which is the most harmful? The previous rules state that the least harmful (or least evil) should be chosen above all others as the primary option. In this case the options as ranked from least to most harmful are as follows:

accidental > poison > lethal injection > hanging > shooting

Depending on the circumstances involved with each option, the order could potentially change (Souryal 2003).

Although rules and formulas will not make the actual decision for a person, they will assist in guiding a person to the best option for given situations.

Result of Decisions

Once a decision is made, it is common for a person to reflect on the decision. Was the right choice made? What would I change? Would I make this decision again? What led me to this decision? It is at this point that we will consider the ethics of means and ends, or what is more commonly known as dilemmas of actions and consequences. Ethical judgment should take human

Table 1.1 Actions and Consequences

	Good Consequences	Bad Consequences
Good actions	Emily takes some extra time to process and collect fingerprints from a secondary room at a crime scene. On examination, it is found that one of those prints belongs to the primary suspect, who had stated that he had never been in the victim's house. The fingerprint evidence ultimately leads to a conviction.	Brody, a questioned documents examiner, decides to set up a pretrial conference with a prosecutor. The meeting is requested in an attempt to clarify the strengths and weaknesses of the document evidence, which is the key evidence in the prosecutor's case. The defense uses the meeting as a means to discredit the expert. Ultimately, the expert is disqualified, and key evidence is thrown out.
Bad actions	Cole is a firearms examiner who gets caught up in questions during his testimony; the questions require more knowledge regarding shooting scene reconstruction. Although Cole is not qualified as an expert in shooting reconstruction, he knows enough to answer the questions. His answers play a major role in the exoneration of the suspect.	Arlene has severe back pain and decides to ingest some of the unknown white powder she is processing. The drug alleviates her pain, which causes her to develop a habit and ultimately costs Arlene her job as a chemist in the crime laboratory.

action into consideration. When actions occur, certain patterns emerge as shown in Table 1.1.

The first two patterns are self-explanatory as these are the outcomes one would expect. The latter are more complex and are better explained with the following examples.

> Madison, a trace evidence examiner, determined that a questioned hair sample should be sent for mitochondrial DNA analysis. Ian, another colleague, agreed with her assessment during his review. When their supervisor, Chad, reviewed the sample, he determined that the hair should actually be sent for nuclear DNA analysis, a more specific test. After showing her that there was excellent sheath material present for the nuclear DNA test, Chad decided to ridicule Madison in front of other colleagues for her initial decision.

This is an example of "bad" actions that led to "good" consequences. Ridiculing a colleague is a troubling action; however, in this case because of Chad's reaction Madison learned that a second review is helpful. She also became aware that she needs to focus on both the quantity and quality of the sheath material present. The bad action is somewhat justified because it had a positive result. What if Chad were not the supervisor? Would this make a difference? What if he had taken it further than ridicule and actually started verbally abusing Madison? Would these factors affect the outcome? The nature of actions, the effectiveness of consequences, and the relationship between the participants factor into making judgments.

> Jake, a crime scene analyst, recently accepted a drug chemist position in his laboratory. His friend Matt, who was already a drug chemist, had recommended Jake for the open position. After a few months in his new job, Jake began to steal small amounts of drugs from evidence for personal use.

This is an example of a "good" action that led to "bad" consequences. Matt's motives were good; he knew his friend was interested and qualified for the position so he wanted to help. The consequences of Jake getting the job were bad because they led to his substance abuse, stealing, and eventual dismissal from the laboratory. Who is to blame? Did Matt have any way to foresee the final outcome? Did Matt fully assess the risk before making a recommendation for his friend? Did Jake have a prior substance abuse problem? If so, did Matt know about it? Did Jake seek this position to support his habit? If there was no prior problem, could Jake have known that drug abuse would occur? In this type of situation, the person who is more informed is the person at fault.

Ethics is involved in many facets of life. Personal ethics are individual in nature, although they need to comingle with professional ethics and the law. People do make honest mistakes and should not be punished for those; however, superiors should conduct a review to assure that the action was unintentional. It is possible for people to make ethical mistakes, so it is important to remember that moral problem solving is an extremely complex process. People do not always arrive at the same conclusion, but that does not necessarily make someone wrong. Although a particular situation might not have one "right" answer, there are clearly many wrong answers. People need to use their best judgment based on personal ethics and common sense. Although using one's best judgment is useful, most people believe that their ethical standards are higher than those of colleagues; unfortunately, many people are wrong! Ethical dilemmas are categorized as situations in which the person did not know the right choice of action, what they considered to be right was too difficult or what was wrong was too tempting. Some examples of these dilemmas include bribery, corruption, gratuities, sex, and perjury. People have different personal obligations set by morals, ethics, law, politics, or religion that can lead to ethical dilemmas. People have various professional obligations that are set by their agency, professional organizations, or accrediting bodies. Due to such obligations defining and dealing with behavior that falls between honest error and fraud is difficult.

Do you think that incompetence is an ethical issue?

The Ethics of the Criminal Justice Culture

2

Introduction

Criminal justice is a broad field relating to the study and application of law to crime. The field spans from prevention of crime to the apprehension of criminals to assistance and rehabilitation postconviction. *Justice* is defined as "equal distribution of society's goods." The principles necessary for distribution of justice are as follows:

1. Principle of the greatest equal liberty: Each and every person should have the right to liberties equal to those of everyone else having the same right (freedoms).
2. Principle of the greatest equal opportunity: The rights of citizens for equal opportunities are not subject to politics or to social interest; they should depend on ability.
3. Difference principle: People accept differences in wealth and privilege; inequalities should be arranged to offer the greatest benefit to the least advantaged (Souryal 2003).

Justice is a primary virtue and should operate as such from the perspective of an unbiased, rational observer. However, it is common that the interpretation of justice impacts, and at times shapes, society. Issues such as abortion, gay marriage, euthanasia, and technology are important social issues that have recently impacted society and the law. Such examples demonstrate the need for features of fairness, equality, and impartiality, which help to describe the criminal justice profession. In addition to police officers, the field includes parole, corrections, and probation officers. The primary focus of the criminal justice profession is police because of the long history and sheer magnitude of this branch of criminal justice. Policing employs many aspects of assistance: Police are to serve, to keep peace, to maintain order, and to protect society, whether the need is crime oriented or service oriented. The public may have varied perceptions of police that stem from the diverse roles of officers in society. Not only are police officers the initiators of the criminal justice process thus entrusted with great power, but they also have the choice not to initiate the criminal justice process. This inaction is illustrated by officers' disregard for particular situations, individuals, or evidence (e.g., "What crack pipe? I didn't see anything"). The appropriate use of power by practitioners reinforces the authority they are given to protect the community and to enforce the laws. Policing is a noble profession that requires exemplary officers. The model officer is flexible, loyal, fair, and skilled in humanity. To achieve quality in criminal justice the primary concerns are social order and moral order. Social order is human concern for legal restrictions and societal standards, such as public safety, freedom, privacy, and good economy. John Rawls's definition of *society* is "the particular individual and government institutions in social agreements." Moral order is human concern for values such as compassion, fairness, and civility. *Values* are defined as "enduring beliefs that a specific mode of conduct or end-state of existence is personally or socially preferable" (Rokeach 1973, p. 5). Criminal justice is an expansive profession whose members hold society's trust to maintain objectivity and fairness.

Recruitment

Criminal justice practitioners endure a great deal of stress inherent to the profession. In addition to dealing with criminals, walking into unknown situations, and not having a rulebook to follow, these men and women are under the pressure of society to behave as model citizens. Fairness, responsibility, and strength are just some of the descriptors used when identifying the character of police officers. There are many reasons someone chooses a career in criminal justice. First, criminal justice practitioners have to be driven from within to act quickly and intelligently, to act with courage, and to recognize the important virtues and traditions of the profession. Next, officers possess a commitment to a noble cause and a desire to make the world a safer place. Finally, police officers' duties are nonroutine, outdoors, dynamic, and socially significant, and they have discretionary decision making, all of which make the profession appealing. The type of person who enters into a law enforcement career may also use influence of the media, as it shapes society's perception of law enforcement as "crime fighters." Policing is considered a subculture within criminal justice. The primary goal of police personnel systems is to find people who are conservative and "traditional": blue-collar, hard-working, middle-class individuals. The selection techniques of law enforcement are based on physical agility, background investigation, polygraph examination, psychological testing, and oral interviews. The most important characteristic is a person's "fit" as an honorable agent of the agency and of the profession. The typical qualities found in law enforcement officers contribute to and exemplify the professional culture of criminal justice.

Culture

Criminal justice, as a culture, is unique. It is based on the thought that people are rational and are able to choose actions freely. If the chosen actions go against standards or laws, society is just in using punishment as a consequence. Police responsibilities increase as social issues intensify and become more complex. Society is very irrational, yet police are required to maintain a positive balance and to address issues that others will not. Teamwork from politicians, legal institutions, the courts, and society are required for law enforcement officials to work successfully. In the times of greatest dissension, police are given the authority and technology to regulate matters yet are commonly left to their own devices because those in power were at a loss as to how to resolve situations. This is just one of the many contradictions involved in policing. Other contradictions include fighting crime to maintain peace, combating unfamiliar and evolving crimes (e.g., methamphetamine labs, computer crimes), and serving society while selectively choosing who to reprimand—for example, three cars are speeding; which should get pulled over? Criminal justice faces issues that directly impact the nature of the profession including its relationship to law, politics, and economics, the nature of punishment coupled with the idea of equality and consistency, and the balance of criminal factors and justice factors in a fair way, regardless of the amount of power provided.

Law enforcement has the duty to uphold democracy. Encarta (Encarta World English Dictionary) defines *democracy* as "the free and equal right of every person to participate in a system of government, often practiced by electing representatives of the people by the majority of the people" and "the control of an organization by its members, who have a free and equal right to participate in decision-making processes." When society is fair and impartial in judgment, justice is done, and society receives the proper distribution of liberties, powers, opportunities, and wealth required to achieve morality, according to Rawls (1971, p. 26). Democracies contain contradictions similar to those mentioned for policing. Some may use such ambiguity as a justification for unethical behavior; however, people should instead attempt to find rational solutions to problems by using the core values of democracy. Human worth, equal opportunity, individualism, access to public communication, access to relevant and accurate information regarding public issues, freedom of choice, acceptance of opposition, honesty in presenting values associated with policies and problems, governmental accountability, honesty in sharing motives and consequences, accuracy, and fairness in providing evidence, and ends not primarily justifying the means encompass the standards of democracy in which society can rely. Democracy in ethics occurs when people live freely despite differences in ideas, cultures, and situational responses. While police agencies aim for effectiveness and follow standards, they must also act fairly and not abuse the power entrusted in them. Concerns about the nature of police power focus on the bigger picture; a person who is arrested for a crime of any magnitude could confront serious, long-term consequences based on the decisions of officers. Consequences may include something as straightforward as a person losing dignity by having a mug shot taken to more severe repercussions such as not being able to secure employment because of a tarnished record stemming from an arrest. The decisions to arrest a person are permanent; police have the power of discretionary procedures known only by police. In this process, the potential for biased judgments occurs while undisclosed to society. Typically, police uphold democracy through ethics, professionalism, and courage.

The professional culture of law enforcement includes some common themes. During a training session police officers were asked to write a one-sentence code of ethics, the five most common themes were legality, service, honesty/integrity, loyalty, and the Golden Rule (Braswell et. al 2008, p. 108). These themes encompass the top dilemmas faced by police. The first dilemma, *discretion*, is the power to make a choice in particularly difficult situations. This is most important when situations have no good solution and no specific law that pertains. The second dilemma is *duty*; this becomes a problem when the official duty of an officer is in question in certain situations or the proper action is not fully applicable to the situation. *Honesty* deals with self-protection, enticements, and the need to affect an arrest. It is not uncommon for officers to have access to money or drugs, both of which could possibly compromise honesty. Honesty is also challenged when someone makes a mistake and needs to explain the situational details to superiors. The final dilemma is *loyalty,* which is related to the wrongdoings of colleagues. Officers facing the common challenges may overcome these with the help of professionalism.

Professionalism is a devotion to duty expressed by people. It is difficult to define because professions are different from occupations, because *professional* is not a constant state, and because professionalism may represent a group as opposed to individuals. Professional groups cannot exist without professionals. Professionals are described as maintaining compassion for people and a sense of legality, honesty, and obligation for the service and duty required by the profession. Police define professionalism as authority, loyalty, and demeanor, which is the "appearance of good" or "looking the part." Sociological factors within the police culture that may influence professionalism include the following:

- Many officers are employed at a young age (18–22 years old), so they may not have familiarity with fair treatment in the workplace.
- Officers commonly come from lower- to middle-class backgrounds.

- Training discusses and advocates democratic ideas but does not effectively demonstrate or reinforce those ideas.
- A large percentage of officers come from military backgrounds; thus, they are rigid with personal ideas and methods of training others.

It is reassuring that the vast majority of police officers are professional, ethical, and dedicated to the goals of fairness and public service.

Ethics of Criminal Justice

Ethics, or rules of principles, are composed of natural law, religious, constitutional, professional, and philosophical principles. While these principles are easily understood, natural law may need further clarification. *Natural law* is the sanction that regulates behaviors of people on the basis of universal traits and common experiences. This law is comparable to common law, civil law, and religious law. Natural law guides natural rights, or human entitlement, such as life, liberty, and freedom. The ethical implication of natural law is to maintain dignity equally, regardless of whether practitioners agree. Criminal justice practitioners should follow the common standards of natural law, including treating people with dignity, governing with reason, not challenging equality of the people, governing people with ethical behaviors that lead to societal contentment, maintaining peace in accordance with the goals of justice, and depending on natural law when formal rules are unavailable. Understanding the concept of natural law allows police to follow the hierarchical order of virtues: human, American, and professional. Human virtues are the highest level and are represented by a dedication to natural law, the service of justice in the interest of society, and the fairness exhibited despite contradicting procedures or pressures. American virtues are the second highest and are composed of a commitment to the Constitution of the United States, including the ideas of liberty, equality, justice, due process, rationality, protection, and accountability. In the criminal justice profession, American virtues are equally important to human virtues. The final virtue is professional and is the lowest ranking because it indicates that a person is part of a profession, which does not necessarily make someone ethical. The hierarchy is helpful when dealing with competing issues. The principles presented provide a basis for ethical behavior in criminal justice.

Ethics is a defining characteristic of the police profession as it consists of the behaviors and attitudes of police officers while acting under the law. It is important to understand the relationship between the law and ethics. Ethics are meant to complement and reinforce the law, not to undermine it. Laws are ever changing, whereas ethics are constant. Laws are logical, reactive instruments of social control, whereas ethics are regulatory and based on reasoning.

Finally, the success of laws is based on procedures and enforcement of rules, whereas the success of ethics is based on knowledge, reason, and kindness. An excellent example of the merger between law and ethics is provided by the U.S. Constitution. It is a guide that provides the truths of social contract for citizens and government. Although the constitutional provisions do not include all moral issues, they are important when discussing ethics in criminal justice because they provide a starting point and state what is "just" and "unjust." Ethics should be carried out by lawmakers, judges, prosecutors, and police officers according to proper practice of the profession. These individuals must have enough knowledge to discern between the ends of justice and the means of justice. The ends of justice refer to the moral responsibility of officers to uphold civic duties, while the means of justice refer to one's concern for rejecting popular justice. To what extent does a morally good end justify an illegal or unethical means? Is overstepping authority to achieve what one perceives as a higher good justified? Answers are difficult because one questions if the decision maker has all of the facts, is able to predict possible ends before choosing means, is aware of all "higher goods," and, finally, if the decision maker is acting in good faith (Souryal 2003).

If ethics is a defining characteristic of the law enforcement profession, it is important to observe how unethical behavior may occur. Police organizations are primarily bureaucratic, formal, and impersonal, which could make for frustrated employees. In addition, mismanagement and discrimination during hiring and promotion are issues that create conflict in agencies. When the officers are unhappy, subcultures within the agency may form and follow beliefs, values, and methods that counter the primary culture. The goal of such subcultures is survival in what is viewed as the larger, more unfair culture of the agency. These subcultures may abuse authority; this can cause resentment among other officers, which could lead to informal coping mechanisms that may eventually lead to unethical behavior. It is often stated by members of subcultures that the public "owes" the police something, when in reality the practitioners are in place to serve the needs of the public. The values of subcultures may often lead to unprofessional or even criminal acts that are justified as legitimate procedure. Examples of actions that are wrong, although justified (by members) within the subculture, include lying to suspects or victims, misuse of authority, perjury as a means to defend a partner, or brutality. Subcultures create obvious professional and ethical problems for an agency. The main ethical objections to occupational subcultures are as follows:

- They violate the ethics of public service and allow for community doubt.
- They undermine the relationship between justice practitioners and clients.

- They allow goals to go unachieved.
- They are conducive to corruption, which could destroy the integrity of an agency.
- They are based on ignorance, bias, and egoism.

Subcultures can tarnish the reputation of an otherwise outstanding agency, including employees who are honest, ethical officers and have no part in the subculture. The awareness of subcultures and the scrutiny that police agencies are under encourage progress in eliminating such groups and maintaining a positive environment. Such steps are a testament to police leaders and managers for instilling positive values while educating employees.

Ethics Training

There are two methods of education within criminal justice agencies: socialization (learned) and culturalization (adopted). More formally, this concept is known as the values-learned perspective, and it argues that police values are not introduced solely by society. Socialization is a process by which practitioners learn ethics through training and practice; this process occurs in many professions including law and medicine. Coursework includes a combination of philosophy and discussion of specific ethical dilemmas relevant to policing. Criminal justice ethics is discussed progressively more as educational standards for police have developed. The increase in standards and education is a positive step for the profession as it enhances credibility and public trust. This more formalized education often comes from experts in the field and veteran officers. Officers are also provided with the reasonable expectations of the field. Although there has been an increase in ethics instruction, the subject is not usually a requirement of formal training programs, thus allowing the subject to be introduced informally. The topic of ethics is learned indirectly in a variety of courses that leads to culturalization. *Culturalization* refers to the more informal means of education based on personal experiences. New recruits learn values informally from their instructors, who were also taught informally. As the pattern of informal education progresses, people's interpretation of the professions' ethical values can become blurred. If an instructor has negative values that conflict with societal or legal values, disservice is done to the students. Although discretion is a common attribute of policing, it could create the potential for problems. Policies and procedure are not extensive enough to regulate every situation officers may encounter. Such "gray areas" where there are no standards require discretionary decision making. How does discretion relate to ethics? Ethical discretion is based on a person's moral commitment to society and the agency in which he or she works. Discretion depends on knowledge, rationality, and devotion to high moral standards. The person should also have the ability to distinguish between shades of gray. For example, an officer pulls someone over for speeding and finds out it is his mother and then lets her go with only a warning. Would the outcome change if the charge were homicide instead of speeding? Would the situation change if the person pulled over had a negative relationship with the officer? The issues to consider when discussing discretion include trust, relationship, and severity of the crime. The discussion should be based on knowledge, rationality, and moral devotion. In situations that call for discretion, officers rely on their inherent, learned, and adopted values that may present the opportunities for unethical behavior.

Unethical Behavior

Though the prevalence and strength of questionable values within the criminal justice system are not as strong today as in the past, some officers still take advantage of their professional position. Despite the *many* officials who cannot be tempted into corruption or portray themselves as anything less than exemplary professionals, the focus here must center on those who act unethically. It is important to explore the perceived rights of officers, the types of misconduct that occur, and the reasons for unethical behavior. Unethical situations may emerge when officers are perceived to have more rights, either by society or by themselves, than the average citizen. One example includes the perceived right of police officers to accept "free coffee or discounted meals" within their districts. Although many business owners (and police for that matter) may simply see this as a method of hospitality, others may disagree. People may question the motives of the business owners (e.g., what do they expect from the officers in return?) or the perspective of the officer (e.g., does he feel that the owner owes him a cup of coffee to patrol the area?), which can lead to mistrust. Another example is the perceived right of officers to enjoy "professional courtesy" when breaking the law. If an off-duty officer is pulled over for speeding, he or she expects that the fellow officer will not ticket him or her as a method of police professionalism. Is this fair? If the person is an officer, he or she should know not to speed in the first place. However, is it because of this professional courtesy that the officer thinks speeding is allowable? Where is the line drawn as far as crimes that go unpunished? The final example is the perceived right of officers to use brutality against suspects or inmates. Though force is often necessary, when does it become excessive? What if the officer justifies his or her actions by stating that the force is used as a means of assisting with rehabilitation? Once again, where is the line drawn regarding how much force is excessive? The perceived rights of officers are transmitted values that may be seen by some as perks of the job, while others feel the actions may contribute to unethical behavior.

There are three main types of unethical behavior in the criminal justice field. This discussion may cause uneasiness; however, the goal is to generate awareness that hopefully will lead to a decrease in problems. The first type, lying and deception, occurs intentionally and is worsened by self-deception and the extent to which a person intends to deceive. Lying is a learned behavior that destroys confidence in a person and may affect anyone. Lies occur by commission or omission (e.g., "If I just don't tell my supervisor that the reagent was bad, she will simply think the test failed"). There are three primary types of lies: helpful lies, teasing lies, and malicious lies. A helpful lie is telling a family that a victim did not suffer before his or her death: It does not change the outcome of the investigation; it simply makes the circumstances more tolerable for the family. An example of a teasing lie or a lie told in jest is when an officer is interviewing an uncooperative, sarcastic suspect and leaves the room saying, "I will be right back; I need to go grab a doughnut." In reality, the officer is not going anywhere; he is giving the suspect time to "stew" but chooses to provide such a lie as he leaves the room. Malicious lies include actions such as planting evidence, perjury, or creating a story to get someone fired. In criminal justice, an officer may coerce a suspect into providing a statement but tell the supervisor that the statement was made of free will. Lying is considered a shameful action even though extenuating circumstances may justify some lies. If a person debates whether to tell a lie, the following guidelines should be considered:

- Are there truthful alternatives? (if so, try those first)
- Will lying produce the same result as the truth? (if so, tell the truth)
- Is the lie a last resort?
- Will a higher moral good be achieved by lying? (e.g., self-defense)

When using the last guideline, it is important that the situation and potential lies are publicly recognized in advance to lessen the chance of people later creating lies to help their cause. So why do people lie? People lie for protection, defense, support, or fun. Institutional lying occurs when professionals deliberately defy an agency's laws, rules, or procedures. During preservice training, officers learn tactical lying, which is encouraged in certain situations and discouraged in others. As one would imagine, the difference in situations may create confusion for trainees. Police learn the value of lying in certain situations that require violation of proper procedure. Situations where the ends seem to justify the means, like gaining access without a proper warrant, using excessive force, or avoiding necessary paperwork, are common problems. In addition, experience may influence officers to lie as they develop coping mechanisms (e.g., excessive alcohol abuse). The need to excuse actions or inactions may alter everyday tasks. Lying is harmful, but in criminal justice it could permanently damage society's trust and create an unsafe environment. Deception should occur only as a last resort in certain cases because the officers' work becomes even more difficult when trust is lost by the public, superiors, coworkers, or informants.

The second primary type of unethical behavior in criminal justice is prejudice and discrimination. *Prejudice* is an adverse judgment or opinion formed without examination of all facts provided or before having sufficient knowledge, whereas *discrimination* is making a distinction based on a behavior pattern. Simply stated, prejudice is an attitude, whereas discrimination is the action resulting from that attitude. Examples of these issues in criminal justice include problems with legal representation of minority groups, bias in processing procedures, lack of language interpreters in court, and limited jobs in criminal justice for minorities. People overcome prejudice by developing sufficient knowledge to resist such negative attitudes. There are two forms of prejudice: culture conditioned and character conditioned. Culture-conditioned prejudice describes sociological prejudice or attitudes that are taught through normal socialization with family, friends, and neighbors, at school, or at church. Character-conditioned prejudice describes psychological prejudice that results from personality features. Although sometimes used synonymously, *stereotyping* is more rigid than prejudice; people are automatically categorized by similarities to a group of people. People who stereotype others exhibit a lack of concern, not a lack of knowledge for differences. Racism is the primary example of prejudice and discrimination. Although racial injustice in the United States is less severe and much more subtle than in the past, it remains a frequent problem. Allegations against police officers are that (1) African Americans are arrested before those of Caucasian descent and (2) more officers are deployed to minority crimes than other crimes. In the correctional system, allegations state that discrimination is so extensive that it is reminiscent of segregation in the 1960s. Primary allegations against parole officers state that African American inmates typically have to appear in front of primarily Caucasian review boards. While laws may subtly reinforce racism, it is helpful if criminal justice professionals use the following facts as moral guidelines in their work:

- Racism is mindless.
- Racism is a contrived social label.
- Racism violates religious principle.
- Racism is constitutionally and legally wrong.
- Racism reflects a person's serious character flaw.
- People deserve equal treatment despite racial differences.
- People deserve treatment as ends rather than means.
- Practitioners should treat members of other races and cultures honorably and generously.

Racial discrimination, which stems from ignorance and indifference, has led to many social problems inside and outside the criminal justice field (Souryal 2003). Laws, policies, and procedures cannot fix the ethical side of discrimination; knowledge is the key to decreasing irrational behaviors, such as prejudice and discrimination. People who are open are better able to gain the knowledge necessary to prevent discrimination.

The final type of unethical behavior commonly found in criminal justice is egoism and abuse of power. *Egoism* is defined by the Oxford English Dictionary (p. 29) as follows:

> The belief, on the part of an individual, that there is no proof that anything exists but his own mind; chiefly applied to philosophical systems supposed by their adversaries logically to imply this conclusion.
>
> The theory which regards self-interest as the foundation of morality. Also, in practical sense: Regard to one's own interest, as the supreme guiding principle of action; systematic selfishness.

It also includes a preoccupation with oneself, an inflated pride, and a gratification in showing others authority in an official position. Egoism reinforces the perspective of "human nature" or a human's act for his or her self-interest. Egoism could lead to an abuse of authority or power. Authority is a person's *right* to control others' behavior and is defined by laws. Power is the *force* practitioners use to control others; as there are no clear rules, a person's power requires justification. Acceptable justification of power is self-defense, support of authority, or that the action occurred within reason and necessity. Responsibility is the balance between authority and power. Ethically, an officer's obligation to follow laws, agency rules, and his or her own reasoning is the most important responsibility, if he or she remains within acceptable limits. Egoism may weaken an officer's responsibility and reduce his or her respect for authority, thus causing a violation of natural law, constitutional law, religious ethics, professional duty, and obligation to ethical codes. Knowing this, how can criminal justice practitioners allow egoism to direct their conduct? People who have power, are vulnerable, and have a great amount of temptation might easily allow such behaviors to occur. Behaviors stem from arrogance, irrationality, and the absence of ethics and are exhibited through brutality, shirking professional obligation, and violating a person's civil rights. Although certain situations may require slight egoism, the unjustifiable examples far outnumber these situations. Any and all unethical behavior within the criminal justice field can damage the core principle of the profession, can provide an "us versus them" mentality with society, can deny citizens of their basic rights, can affect social order, can discredit practitioners' ability to remain faithful to their duties, and may encourage corruption.

Despite the negative outcomes and the public backlash created when those in the criminal justice field are unethical, it still occurs. Why? Primary reasons for unethical behavior are categorized under the headings *opportunity* and *incentive*. Opportunity includes the potential for corruption. *Corruption* is the intentional violation of organizational norms by public employees for personal gain and ranges from theft of drugs or money to criminal conspiracy for drug trafficking. Corruption may occur as a result of officers' discretionary decisions. Unless an officer has strong character and beliefs, is truthful no matter what, and is fully guided by self-respect and excellence, there is a potential for corruption. Discretionary decisions encourage unethical behavior when temptations are involved. Officers should have awareness that there is a very fine line between acceptable and unethical practices in policing. Temptations such as money, drugs, cars, and power are incentives for unethical behavior. Political power within the profession is also an incentive or a source of pressure for officers. When ethical principles and codes have been introduced as work strategies, officers have called them "unworkable" and "naïve" because such principles are equated with weakness in this professional culture (Souryal 2003).* Does this mean that there are no principles or codes in place? No, many agencies have ethical codes of conduct that they follow. However, this means either that the codes in place may not be as thorough as in other professions or that the codes are not being strictly followed by practitioners. Criminal justice agencies are in charge of justice for society so they should act fairly; when they do not, it could have a profound negative impact on society. Although the frequency of unethical situations is not as high as it was in the past, how officers react to questionable situations, values, or decisions is described by Braswell and McCarthy as their *moral career*. Whether reacting positively or negatively, where should the blame fall for officers who partake in unethical behavior within the profession?

The blame for unethical behavior in criminal justice gets evenly distributed, depending on whose opinions are asked. Some people accuse the nature of *the system* because, historically, police were considered ethical if they achieved the desired end of "getting the bad guy off the street." Corrupt people tend to blame the system; ideas can be slanted or misinterpreted by officials, and those individuals influence the integrity of the government. An example of this is provided by slavery in the United States; although it was the norm at the time, not everyone was influenced, and those uninfluenced citizens eventually helped to overcome the injustice. *Pressure* is a commonly cited factor. When police officers make a mistake they are scrutinized more so than lawyers, media personnel, or most other professionals because more is at stake (e.g., someone being wrongly accused of rape could have severe

---

* Souryal, S. 2003 *Ethics in Criminal Justice: In Search of the Truth* (3rd Edition). Albany, NY: Matthew Bender & Company, Inc., a member of the Lexis Nexis Group.

consequences for the victim, the suspect, and the families and friends of those individuals). Probation and patrol officers have the same roles as police and correctional officers but have the added responsibilities of extensive reporting, huge caseloads, and continual paperwork. *Temptations* such as adaptation to pressure, convenience, and bureaucracy affect practitioners. Although the vast majority of police acknowledge and support the ethical components of the job, some find the temptation of working so close to "the dark side" of society too much to handle without surrendering to it. If checks and balances are faulty, the range of unrestricted powers might create a solution that makes it easy for someone to make bad decisions. *Power* is another factor responsible for unethical behavior in criminal justice. Police agencies' abuse of power may stem from being the biggest, most armed, most expensive, and most unrestricted entity in society. This differs from some other pressures because professional power is outside the control of individual police officers. What is in the control of officers is how they handle the power bestowed on them. *Camaraderie* is a factor many people might not consider. It has been shown that superiors may tolerate or even encourage unethical behavior among their staff if they themselves have overstepped boundaries at one time or another. Agencies with *alternate agendas* may require some blame for unethical behaviors. Politically motivated agencies, agencies that enforce quotas, and agencies that encourage competition within its practitioners add to professional pressure. The resulting stress may lead to misbehavior and the crossing of ethical lines. Finally, a lack of concern by superiors influences unethical behavior. For example, as long as legal and administrative duties are done, people choose not to concern themselves with moral issues, especially if they are not directly impacted. These factors are the primary source of blame for unethical behavior in the criminal justice professions.

Sources of Pressure for the Forensic Scientist

Forensic scientists are subject to pressures from four distinct sources:

1. The *police* who are usually our clients.
2. The *adversary system,* which will evaluate our data.
3. The *science* on which our data are based.
4. Sometimes, our *personal* sense of ethics and morals.

Law enforcement creates challenges for the forensic scientist for a variety of reasons. The first factor is the obligation to follow the law. Both groups are required ethically to preserve the integrity of the investigation and of the agency; however, law enforcement has the goals to protect, serve, and "get the bad guy," whereas the scientist's goal is to conduct tests, to interpret results, and to explain them in reports. Next, law enforcement has no obligation to remain impartial or to disclose all information, whereas the scientists' role is to remain unbiased and to provide all information. Officers may not collect all relevant physical evidence at a crime scene due to lack of training, lack of time, lack of knowledge regarding proper procedures, or intentionally. These factors reflect the expectations of law enforcement compared with those of forensic scientists.

Based on the differences in cultures, do forensic scientists have an ethical obligation toward the actions of law enforcement? *No, forensic scientists are not responsible for police practices.* However, it is in scientists' best interest to familiarize themselves with the common differences. Police learn the ethics of law enforcement in one of two ways: in a low-pressure environment such as the police academy or under pressure while on the job. There are pros and cons to each of these methods; police need to find a balance between the two extremes. When a person is free from pressure, objectivity and open-mindedness are more likely to occur; however, this does not accurately portray the working conditions of law enforcement officers. One of the first sources of on-the-job pressure for new officers begins with training. After the police academy, much of the training occurs through socialization on the job. Such informal training encourages rookies to adopt and adapt to the rules, values, and attitudes of the agency or their mentors. Socialization creates situations where questions posed by rookies regarding proper procedures could receive responses such as, "That is the way it has always been done." These examples are not limited to police rookies, as they may also apply to young forensic scientists or anyone else in a trainee-type position. The bottom line is that police are an essential part of the criminal justice system. Society relies on police to act ethically, though they may or may not feel an ethical responsibility toward the scientists with whom they work. For forensic professionals (e.g., law enforcement) to maintain ethical practices they should stay current in new policies and procedures, insist on acquiring appropriate samples, reject improper requests, and report suspected negligence. Conclusions drawn by the forensic examiner in the laboratory should be based on the scientific evidence and not on information from field investigation. A good example of how the cultures of law enforcement and forensic science vary is that it is acceptable for a law enforcement officer to act on information received from another officer; however, it is unethical for a scientist to arrive at a conclusion in the absence of proper evidence or data. Although the law enforcement profession adds pressure for forensic scientists, officers have a great deal of pressure as well. Such pressures are easier to handle when each "side" has a basic understanding of the differing cultures and perspectives of the two fields.

Ethics in the Courtroom
The Scientist's Perspective
3

Introduction

Law and forensic science are complementary yet contradictory professions. The challenges come from the differences in the inherent nature of the two cultures including overall function, value, and goals. Like the differences between forensic science and criminal justice, each group has its own standards for conduct, beliefs, and obligations.

Each profession has objections. Forensic scientists often find fault in the unethical conduct of aggressive attorneys, even though the attorney is fulfilling his or her duty of representing the client's best interests. Conversely, attorneys are often frustrated by scientists who may not provide conclusive evidence. Table 3.1 shows the primary differences between the two cultures.

How should attorneys and scientists bridge the communication gaps within the court system? Mandatory disclosure of all scientific evidence *before* a trial would result in better information being provided to the triers-of-fact (or the judge and jury). It is important to keep in mind that miscommunication in the courtroom may have irreversible consequences to the case, the lawyers, the experts, and, most importantly, the victims and the defendant. Information that is ethically important may not be possible to disclose during the course of expert testimony; experts need to have an awareness of the rules governing their testimony to provide information that, while ethically necessary, may not be legally warranted. Communication regarding experts may center on their qualifications including education, training,

Table 3.1 Differences of Cultures: Science and the Law

Issue	Science	Law
Truth	Serves the interest of itself	Serves the interest of the client
Communication	Open	Privileged
Process	Unbiased and systematic	Adversary
Goals	• Provide socially valued goods and services • Advance human knowledge • Eliminate false beliefs • Documentation	• Serve the client • Produce a better argument than the opposing counsel

and experience. The only acceptable substitute for peer review in the judicial system is the critique of an expert's analysis by the opposing side's expert. Arguably this is not always an ideal situation, depending on the qualifications and experience of the other side's expert. The final and most important step toward better communication is realizing that bias exists. To overcome bias and to better serve the parties involved, the court could require the forensic scientist to present testimony for the side *not* retaining his or her services. Also, an expert may advise the court directly (instead of or in addition to other experts) upon the judge's request. The concern in this case is that the expert is then granted more "weight" because of his or her lack of vested interest, which could create a false sense of security that there is no bias. These steps may possibly decrease gaps in communication while allowing the cultures of science and the law to coexist.

The key to overcome contradictions between professional cultures is balance. It is quite possible to work within the guidelines set forth by both professions when there is mutual respect, honesty, and an understanding of the other culture. The means to understanding differences is the realization that the scientist has a duty to describe the evidence as it is whereas the attorney has a duty to describe the evidence in the most favorable light for his or her client. The intricacies of the relationship between law and forensic science are further examined through the roles each plays in the judicial system.

Role of Attorneys

The role of attorneys is to facilitate justice for a client. Attorneys portray their role in a variety of ways—most commonly the legal advocate, the counselor, or the friend. First, the legal advocate is what most people commonly perceive as an attorney's role. This category includes the attorney that follows the clients' requests despite whether their actions are considered moral or good. The attorney does not contribute his or her ethical stance to the client or case. Next, the counselor or guru attorney is in the position to advise clients of appropriate actions. This attorney is also categorized as a moral agent. The last category is the friend or client-centered attorney. The attorney in this role persuades clients not to engage in inappropriate and, most importantly, unethical acts. Although it is common for people to regard prosecutors as advocates for justice and defense attorneys as advocates for their clients, both attorneys must be moral agents. As "moral agents," attorneys impose their personal view of ethics into their activities for the client. Prosecutors have additional ethical requirements as moral agents. Prosecutors are public servants who, because of the rules for discovery, have no responsibility for confidentiality. The goal of the prosecutor is to act in the interests of the state in criminal matters, specifically the prosecution of said matters. There is a great deal of literature on the role attorneys should play and the ethics of law, but this unfortunately does not decrease the potential for misconduct inherent to the profession. Both prosecutors and defense attorneys may employ unethical behavior such as selectively choosing jurors, coaching witnesses, and misusing experts. In addition, the prosecution should exhibit caution with issues specific to their professional role. The ability to control plea bargains, to file charges at their discretion, to select cases to prosecute, to terminate "weak" cases, and to make promises in exchange for testimony could lead to unethical behaviors by prosecutors. Attorneys must maintain an objective standard of justice and strike a professional balance between the clients' interests and the law (Condlin 2003).

> What actions (if any) should an attorney take when representing a person or a group with conflicting values to his or her own?

Attorneys who choose to act as moral agents for their clients may follow basic principles. Those principles, as presented by Cohen (1991), include treating people as ends and not simply means to winning a case, treating clients and others in a comparable manner, not misleading the court, willingly sacrificing for just causes, not exchanging money for wrongful purposes, avoiding harm of others, showing loyalty to the client, and acting consistently on one's own ethical judgment. The principles allow attorneys to act independently to determine appropriate actions. In addition to the informal principles, Memory and Rose (2002) state that attorneys are guided by formal principles in the form of the American Bar Association's Model Rules of Professional Conduct. Cohen disagrees, citing that the rules do not prevent all acts that are unethical and immoral; for example, they do not prevent attorneys from remaining silent when a third party is harmed. Cases that support Cohen's perspective include the Enron and WorldCom business examples. The Model Rules for Professional Conduct prohibit illegal and unethical behaviors while still allowing attorneys to act as advocates for clients. If followed, the rules assist attorneys in becoming effective and ethically "good" in their role. Updated in 2002, the rules address client–lawyer relationships, integrity of the profession, courtroom behavior, conflicts of interest, use of media, relationships with other lawyers, and much more. As an example, the rules dictate that an attorney should tolerate clients' decisions regarding the objectives of his or her representation, should not assist the client in criminal or deceptive behavior, and must have informed consent to discuss clients' cases with anyone other than the clients. The rules are enforced by a committee on ethical responsibility, and, in addition, each state bar association enforces its own rules. In their role, attorneys should act as moral agents.

Attorney–Expert Relationship

The role of the attorney is quite different from the role of the forensic expert witness. Attorneys are advocates, whereas experts are educators. As advocates, attorneys are often perceived negatively by the public, especially regarding their honesty. How then do the roles overlap? Attorneys are to ask questions, while experts are to answer those questions. Attorneys may attempt to discredit the expert, while experts are to remain calm and to report findings and provide opinions. Attorneys are supposed to support the expert, while experts are to support the scientific information by providing it in an unbiased manner. It is the duty of the attorney to avoid weakening the expert's objectivity, to respect the boundaries of each professional position, and to allow the expert sufficient time to review the case.

Ethically, attorneys should review potential questions with the expert before the trial or deposition, should not pick and choose which records or details to provide to the expert, and should defend the expert they have retained to the best of their ability. When selecting private scientific experts, attorneys should choose experts that are reputable, objective, current in their field, willing to testify for either the prosecution or defense, and have opinions that are consistent with the relevant information. If a private expert feels that he or she cannot work within the attorney's theory or position, he or she should completely remove himself or herself from the case, not simply switch sides. Expert witnesses and attorneys should prepare for court by discussing the evidence, either with a pretrial conference or a phone call. During this preparation, attorneys and experts review facts and prior statements and discuss issues pertinent to the case. Attorneys should listen to experts' suggestions regarding their expertise because the experts may have better ways to explain or present things. It is important that the expert fully understands the questions attorneys ask before answering and does not provide more information than the question warrants. If the attorney is familiar with the opposing counsel, he or she may prepare the expert to "read" the attorney and to discuss what that attorney typically focuses on, such as they commonly attack experts' qualifications and/or the methods used. The relationship between the experts and attorneys should remain open and available to either side. The best experts consider all facts and data, are able to logically counter points made by opposing experts if necessary, are able to recognize limitations of the science, of the evidence, and of their knowledge, and, most importantly, never compromise scientific objectivity.

Experts may face pressures uncommon to their daily lives but common to the judicial environment and in court. It is important to note that adaptation to pressure does not equate yielding to it. Modern judges, juries, and attorneys may suspect experts' roles because in the past experts were part of the criminal justice system. Such experts may have exhibited bias or advocacy, wanted to please their employers, were not sure of their exact role, were not always honest, and may have had problems with confidentiality. In the late 1800s and early 1900s scientists became routinely employed as experts. This association gave experts the reputation of being advocates. Some common signs of advocacy include experts making statements that they "cannot be wrong"; experts who do not describe evaluation procedures or do not bring data, material, or the results of examinations to court; and experts who make personal attacks on opposing witnesses. A consequence of commonly being called by one side (no matter which side) is the pressure caused to the experts, including the following:

- Preparation of reports containing minimal information.
- Reporting findings without an interpretation.
- Omitting a significant point from a report.
- Failure to report or acknowledge any weakness.
- Failure to differentiate between opinions based on experiment and opinions based on experience.
- Expressing an opinion with greater certainty than the data justify.

Pressures may lead to problems when the expert is invited to strategy sessions, asked to assist in the impeachment of experts testifying for the opposing side, or asked to sit with council and assist with cross-examination of opposing experts. In general, expert witnesses have a greater impact in court than other witnesses and definitely impress juries. The recent growth of forensic science and the acceptance by the legal system reflect society's trust in science and technology. Society believes physical evidence and scientific testimony are more reliable than other forms of evidence. The information regarding forensic science is compelling if it is presented correctly and accurately. Many people in the forensic community have stated that in their experience, juries want a "TV-like" trial where DNA and fingerprints are always available, which poses the question:

> Do you think juries find accuracy compelling or do they find the type of evidence compelling?

One attorney has stated, "Many trials are a battle among experts." Some judges feel that experts confuse the jury, especially if both sides have their own expert. Experts may offer testimony that is not the exact truth but has the best statistics. Such half-truths may be told for a variety of reasons, such as to receive a good evaluation, to receive funding, or to please the attorney.

No matter the reason, the actions that result from common pressures are not appropriate and reflect badly on the scientific profession.

Ethical dilemmas will occur, but what steps could attorneys and expert witnesses take to eliminate, or at least lessen, issues? If forensic scientists or attorneys were required to reveal evidence developed in the investigative stage, the administration of justice may be enhanced. Since the court, prosecution, and the defense are calling experts, the technical quality and ethics of testimony need to increase. Experts have the right to limit themselves to consultant tasks to avoid ethical conflict, if they feel such action is necessary. Although the cultures of the judicial system and forensic science vary, these actions toward mutual cooperation may help to decrease the potential for ethical dilemmas.

Misconduct

After examining the roles of the attorney and the expert witness, how do the professional cultures collide? Where does misconduct occur and how? Misconduct comes in the form of fraud, false promises, or threats. Many ethical dilemmas are a direct result of the conflicting obligations inherent to practicing law. Other types of misconduct include ignoring, misrepresenting, or misusing scientific evidence. Forensic evidence is misused when biased experts are hired, test results are suppressed, or expert findings are overstated. If these facts are known, why is no one working to change such a negative perspective? Frankly, misbehavior by prosecutors (or anyone) happens both because it works and because they do not get caught. When the prosecution has a strong opening statement, raises arguments with the opponent's case, or has evidence stricken, the person's confidence and performance level increases. Typically, the prosecutor is seen as the "good guy," and this adds to the attorney's feeling of empowerment. History shows through examples like the O. J. Simpson trial that the stronger the case, the more the prosecutor is able to get away with in the courtroom. Additionally, prosecutors are not personally liable for misconduct because it is the "nature of the beast."

Experts may face a number of problems after agreeing to testify, including the following:

- Resisting attorneys who want testimony that supports their client's position.
- Evaluations that prove disadvantageous to the side that has retained them.
- Being approached for a combination of advice, evaluations, and expert testimony (i.e., private experts).
- Attorneys who waste time.

- Experiencing inconvenience or pressure by attorneys, agencies involved, the clients or their family, the court schedule, travel, or accommodations.
- Having opinions distorted and their reputation impugned.
- Having testimony countered by an expert who is not on their level of expertise but is still viewed by the court as an expert (e.g., federal agents, police officers).
- Unethical to make negative comments about them.
- Many scientists will refuse to testify in this situation.

The first area of misconduct stems from conflicts of interest. *Conflicts of interest* are behaviors or actions involving personal gain or financial interest. Such conflicts undermine or impair a person's ability to make reliable and objective decisions. For example, an expert may have prior knowledge of the case or an association with people involved, the outcome may directly impact the expert financially, or the relationship with another expert may impact the case. No conflict of interest or perceived conflict should exist between the expert and the retaining attorney because this could possibly compromise objectivity and honesty while undermining the expert's credibility. Conflicts (or potential conflicts) need to be disclosed to all relevant parties before expert testimony is given. Limits have been established in laws, guidelines, and regulations that define the level of financial interest that creates conflicts of interest; however, there is little recognition of a hierarchy of damage done to the public well-being. For instance, there is greater harm when conflicts of interest influence evidence directly versus the conflict of purchasing instrumentation from a particular vendor. Actions viewed as conflicts of interest vary by state and federal statutes, case law, contracts, professional standards, and agreements between parties. Although many codes prohibit activities that create an appearance of conflicts, there is no general agreement about the circumstances that create a true scientific conflict of interest. Apparent conflicts should be monitored closely because they can become a real conflict if the person's interests change. Conflicts of interest in science are especially disturbing because they have the potential to compromise objectivity of scientific judgment. It is important to avoid all potential types of conflict to assure the utmost credibility for the scientist, the work, and the profession.

Another area of potential misconduct concerns the experts' reports. Attorneys may request that experts not write reports because they know the information is discoverable and do not want to risk potentially helping the opposing attorney. If an expert is asked to change words in a report for purposes of clarifying technical information, he or she should assure that it does not alter the content. If the expert finds errors in a report, he or she should add an amended page, cross out the incorrect portion, or produce a corrected version while maintaining the original in the case file. An expert must exhibit caution when attorneys request he or she alter reports. Suggestions might include omitting details or simply revising points. Either way, such a request creates the impression of advocacy on the part of the expert, which could lead the triers-of-fact to deem him or her as untrustworthy.

Although the remaining areas of potential misconduct are infrequent, they do occur due to inappropriate motivation. The first example, intentionally inaccurate expert testimony, may occur for the protection or help of friends that are in the role of attorney, plaintiff, or defendant. Additional motivations for inaccurate testimony include personal disputes with attorneys or opposing experts, incompetence, and outcome-based compensation. There is a difference between someone called to testify because he or she is reliable, honest, and professional versus the "professional testifier" or "whore." The latter include people who are typically the yes-men and may be seduced into manipulating testimony. The professional testifier may also have a good deal of free time either because he or she is retired or is a professional consultant; both cases might yield an income-driven motivation for providing testimony. Model Rules for Professional Conduct (American Bar Association, 2002), Rule 3.4, states, in essence, that attorneys cannot obstruct access to evidence or alter, destroy, or conceal any materials having potential evidentiary value. If the attorney knows testimony is false, he or she must ethically refuse to offer such testimony in trial, but if he or she "reasonably believes" the testimony is false, then it must be offered. Defense attorneys must ethically question a prosecutor's witness, challenge technicalities, and question physical evidence in an attempt to create reasonable doubt for the triers-of-fact. Misconduct is more likely to occur when diverse cultures coexist; it is important to have awareness of common issues to prevent future incidents.

Examples of Misconduct

It is expected that examples of misconduct in the court system are relatively low considering the amount of time spent covering ethical matters in law schools. However, lawyers are prime targets for the public's mistrust. Although defense attorneys typically have worse reputations, prosecutors are not exempt from unethical behavior. Gershman (2003) writes about prosecutors who misuse forensic evidence by suppressing the evidence, by calling on incompetent or biased experts, by rejecting exculpatory reports, or by overstating findings. "Some prosecutors lied out of personal ambition, some out of zeal to protect society, but most lied because they had gotten caught up in the competition to win" (Wishman 1981, p. 52–53). Although complaints against prosecutors are rare, when they occur it is typically very scandalous. Politics, community, and media influence contribute to potential misconduct. Rampant media attention causes the public to focus on and to question the judicial system. The following examples will shed some light onto unethical prosecutors.

Duke Lacrosse Case, 2006

Michael Nifong was the elected official who charged three Duke lacrosse players of raping a young woman (AP 2007b, Wilson 2007, Wilson & Barstow 2007). The prosecutor was up for reelection that year, so he thrived on the media attention. There were many public appearances and statements made regarding the suspects and the alleged evidence. The evidence Nifong discussed in statements was actually false. The three suspects were Caucasian, and the accuser was African American; at first people believed it was a case of racism. The men tried to prove their innocence by voluntarily providing DNA samples for testing. Families of the young men felt not only like they were hostages of the situation but also that the prosecutor chose to believe the lies of a young woman to advance his political career. So what happened? A forensic expert for the prosecution admitted that he and the district attorney had DNA evidence that could exonerate the defendants but did not report it. Dr. Brian Meehan was hired by Nifong to conduct DNA testing. His results showed that the DNA on the rape kit matched four unidentified men, none of whom were the lacrosse players. Although a report was issued, potentially exculpatory information was left out. This was a blatant violation of professional standards that launched investigations into the company for which Meehan worked. At a hearing, Meehan testified that he and Nifong agreed to limit the report to the evidence that matched the lacrosse players or three of the accuser's friends. He did provide his results to Nifong *before* the report was issued but also said that Nifong did not specifically request exclusion or inclusion of the information. The district attorney is required by law to disclose information to the defense regarding evidence. In this case, Nifong did not disclose all information until he was court ordered to do so approximately six months after receiving the information from Meehan. In addition, Nifong told the court that he was "not aware of any additional information" that could have been exculpatory. The district attorney believed, and stated, that he was part of the solution not the problem because he discussed the evidence (even though Nifong mentioned it after Meehan testified regarding the existence of such evidences). Upon admitting that he was aware of the findings, Nifong stated that the nondisclosure was simply an oversight.

Even though the initial rape allegations were dropped, the case was transferred from county to state jurisdiction. In April 2007, the attorney general of North Carolina, Roy Cooper, dropped all charges against the men for lack of evidence (and because the evidence that did exist was exculpatory). Nifong was later highly criticized in the media and underwent an investigation by the North Carolina State Bar for dishonesty, fraud, and deceit. More specifically, the bar directed the investigation toward Nifong's suspected participation in prejudicial actions and for supposedly conducting the investigation with dishonesty, fraud, deceit, or misrepresentation. So what were the major issues? First, Nifong used the case as a means to an end; reelection was his *personal gain*. Second, he showed *bias,* as he called the men "children of privilege" and made the crime about race. Third, there was an *abuse of power* demonstrated by Nifong's unjustified arrest and zealous prosecution. Next, he was *deceitful* in having hidden facts about the DNA evidence that could have exonerated the men. Due to the hidden evidence and information, Nifong denied the lacrosse players *due process*. In addition, his media appearances could be considered highly prejudicial. Finally, in denying the men due process, Nifong *neglected his duties* as prosecutor and as an elected official. In addition to the prior reasons, Nifong never reviewed the evidence, nor did he ever personally interview the victim. The prosecution of the men continued even after the evidence disappeared. In June 2007, Nifong resigned and was then disbarred by North Carolina.

Federal Prosecutors, 2007

Federal prosecutors are political appointees of the president, so dismissal based on politics is not unordinary. In 2007, the U.S. attorney general, Alberto Gonzales, dismissed seven federal prosecutors, citing "performance matters" as the reason (Zajac 2007, Cohen 1991). It was later discovered that the firings were politically driven; the George W. Bush administration wanted "more loyal" prosecutors. Critics were skeptical of the motivation behind the firing because they saw it instead as a punishment for investigating Republican (but not Democratic) officeholders. Gonzales countercharged that the prosecutors in question were lax in pursuing immigration cases and other Bush administration priorities. No matter which side was correct, the case itself raised important ethical considerations. Although federal prosecutors are political appointees and serve at the pleasure of the president, the oath that is sworn on makes their first obligation to the U.S. Constitution. This oath allows prosecutors to maintain due process of the laws that govern the United States. Loyalty to the administration comes second behind the responsibility of upholding Constitutional rights. Until this point in history, because of that traditional circumspection, U.S. attorneys have been replaced en masse only at the beginning of a new presidential administration. Gonzales could have maintained the tradition of reserve by declining the firings as an overextension; instead he apologized only for handling the matter so poorly that the prosecutors' firing had become a public issue. Gonzales seemed intent on making sure the situation was viewed as a precedent. He and future attorneys general can make sure prosecutors yield to the administration's priorities or that they at least factor political considerations to deliberations (Zajac 2007). So what did Gonzales have to say about the exodus? He told the Senate Judiciary Committee (Lilly 2007):

> What we're trying to do is ensure that for the people in each of these respective districts, we have the very best possible representative for the Department of Justice. I would never, ever make a change in a United States attorney for political reasons or if it would in any way jeopardize an ongoing serious investigation. I just would not do it.

Factors to consider in the example of the case of the federal prosecutors include actions, motives, and responsibilities. This case provides an example of perception, duty, and abuse of power. Though the situation may have met standards of conduct, the perception is that there was more to the story. What is the duty of the federal prosecutors? Who decides when they have not maintained the duty? Who is responsible for enforcing the governing principles? When should the individual or entity responsible for managing the prosecutors be called into question?

Research Ethics in Science

4

> There are no forbidden questions in science, no matters too sensitive or delicate to be probed.
>
> **Carl Sagan**

Introduction

Scientific knowledge is derived from observation, study, and experimentation. Science is systematic and exact and follows a scientific method. The basic steps are as follows:

1. Ask a question or pose a research problem based on initial data and background knowledge.
2. Develop a working hypothesis based on existing information.
3. Make predictions from the hypothesis and background knowledge.
4. Test hypothesis; collect additional data.
5. Analyze data.
6. Interpret data.
7. Confirm or disconfirm hypothesis. Cannot be proven, just supported or refuted.
8. Disseminate results.

Henry H. Bauer's (1994) *Scientific Literacy and the Myth of the Scientific Method* states that science rarely proceeds in such a systematic way as the scientific method implies. The reasoning behind this is that the process of science uses many strategies and methods as it goes; it is not an orderly process. The steps of the scientific method provide an ideal, not a specific formula. Solving problems and answering questions use a combination of theory, observation, and experimentation. Using one scientific method can give society unrealistic expectations of science and scientists; it is important to remember that science is the work of humans and that humans are impressionable, impulsive, subjective, and capable of rationalization. In addition, humans have accountability in acquiring funds, justifying actions, and explaining outcomes to the public. Basic human values shape the direction of science, as science is built on trust and honesty. It is "a profession in which individuals cooperate together in order to advance human knowledge, eliminate ignorance, and solve practical problems" (Resnik 1998).

According to David Goodstein's (2002, p. 71) "Myth of the Noble Scientist" idea, scientists are guilty of promoting, or at least tolerating, a false image of ourselves. His implication is that integrity presents an image of perfection. Unfortunately, this image does science a disservice because human behavior is a considerable factor in science. Science is unique in that it is both a profession and a social institution, which is not always the case in other fields. Certain criteria distinguish professions from social institutions. Professions enable people to obtain socially valued goals and to incorporate professional obligations to assure goals are met. Professions have standards of competence and conduct, require formal and informal training and education, include governing bodies for ensuring professional standards are met, are granted certain privileges to provide socially valued goods and services, and are often recognized as intellectual authorities. Science does not fit the criteria perfectly, but well enough for consideration as a profession. So how did science become a profession? The answer is through societies, journals, universities, research, education, employment in military and industry, technological applications, and public recognition. The goals of science include advancing human knowledge through problem solving, eliminating false beliefs, seeking truths, and providing justification and evidence for ideas. The scientist should value openness, free inquiry, and free exchange of ideas to accomplish the goals of science.

Science, Technology, and Society

Society greatly shapes the public's perception of scientific matters. The general thought about science is that the profession is not responsive to society's needs; the process of answering questions and meeting needs takes too long. The public's view regarding the length of time science takes to provide answers is especially prevalent in forensic science as television shows like *CSI: Crime Scene Investigation* emerge. People expect results immediately. The general public expects science to remain unbiased and not become overly politicized. When scientific opinions are swayed by politics, public opinion of science decreases. It has been shown that trust between science and society has declined in the last decade. Society questions the changing opinions of science regarding important issues such as stem cell research, overuse of medications like antibiotics, and awareness of cancer-causing agents. Society may also distrust science because unethical behaviors that contribute to mistrust are often reported by the media. Society has granted the scientific community with privileges that are upheld as the public invests confidence into the profession.

To combat negative opinions that society holds of science, scientists should understand their different roles in society to better understand how to positively shape the public's perception. In addition, the public needs to be educated as well as protected from "junk science" and misinformation. People may fear scientific information and become frustrated when facts are deemed inaccurate. Junk science, or science that is not consistent with generally accepted scientific views, needs to be eliminated from society, although that is not entirely possible. It is possible, however, to filter scientific findings through peer review, publication, and repeatability of the procedure to decrease the frequency of junk science. Although the public realizes that differences in the interpretation of data and honest errors occur, the variation in results and opinions is still confusing. Secrecy and competition contribute to a loss of public confidence in the integrity of science. Scientists receive criticism for the lack of information they provide to the public even if the lack of details may occur as a "safeguard." It is important to protect the public from junk science to assure that real scientific information is respected and valued.

One of the foremost convictions in science is open communication. The media has a large influence on the public perception of science. Science communicates with the public through media such as books, newspapers, television media, science fiction, and magazines. Although science and media have the same duty to gather information, to provide accurate and objective facts, and to sustain social responsibility, the two cultures have different standards, methods, goals, competencies, and funding sources. Communications between the scientific community and the media should help to foster the public's knowledge, not promote distrust of science. At times, interactions between the cultures of science and the media may have unintended and adverse consequences for the public. In science, peer review and publication are important to maintain the confidence provided by the public as well as other scientists. There are a variety of scientific meetings where scientists present findings to their peers. However, it is important that scientists are aware that such meetings are often open to the public, including the media. This is not to say that research presented at scientific meetings is inaccurate, however; there may be reasons the research is not yet published. For example, preliminary results presented to a small audience provide the scientific community with general information regarding the research that is occurring, not necessarily a complete conclusion. Also, a scientist may present controversial work at a meeting to establish the extent of debate the research creates. The potential for misquotes is another reason for scientists to realize that meetings are open to the public. It is much easier for misquotes in the media to occur from a public presentation than it is from a journal article, as most presentations are not prewritten, edited material.

Communication is extremely valuable in science as long as the potential downsides are considered. Scientists often seek media coverage for discoveries because they want the public to know what is happening or they hope to gain support for the research. In particular, scientists have an obligation to raise public consciousness because the public has the potential to make important contributions to science and technology. Open communication with a high degree of intellectual freedom allows research to flourish; debates are an excellent means for this type of open communication. To prevent potential attacks and to strengthen the research, debates are useful. Communication is a valuable part of scientific research.

Research and Publication

Scientific research is the process of weighing and balancing objectives and motivations to advance knowledge and the understanding of human behavior. Standards of research, such as honesty, integrity, and objectivity, are the foundation for conducting science. In the course of scientific research, scientists must choose what problems to study, what methods to use, what literature to cite, how to collect and organize data, how to interpret and report data, and how much time to allocate for the various duties. Typically, the scientists' time and effort get distributed among teaching, managing, and coordinating research, identifying new problems, interpreting data, publicizing advances and achievements, and, most importantly, searching for funds to support research. The decision regarding how to distribute time and effort are influenced by employers, potential rewards, and personal qualities. Scientists must constantly balance the demands of science with their personal and professional ethics. Typically, research is not a well-organized and fully planned process; it is aided by luck, intuition, and unexpected discoveries. Although ideal research is untainted by prejudice, the process is conducted by humans so by nature it is not ideal. "Scientific certainty" and the level of certainty are limited because it is an individual's best evaluation of a given matter. Researchers often have a variety of backgrounds and motivations that influence their work. Even actions that are justified by scientific inquiry may have started because of personal gain. Unfortunately, scientific research may carry economic rewards that may skew some people's results. When studying scientific research it is important to keep an open mind while considering the researcher's possible biases.

Research builds on earlier work done by others. Oftentimes, research groups at universities are the backbone of science, but can those institutions be relied on? The integrity of colleagues and the reliability of the data are extremely important to justify time, allocation of money, and resources available for further research. To assure that honesty and integrity are upheld in research, science uses peer review and publication as a system of checks and balances. Though peer review is required in the process of scientific research, it has limitations and should not create a false sense of security regarding scientific findings. Potential problems with peer review include the inaccessibility of original data, bias by reviewers, and time or knowledge constraints. As Arnold S. Relman, editor of the *New England Journal of Medicine*, states regarding trust in scientific research, "It seems paradoxical that scientific research, in many ways the most questioning and skeptical of human activities, should be dependent upon personal trust. But the fact is that without trust the research enterprise could not function" (Djerassi 1991). Honesty in scientific research is quite important and helps prevent some of the potential problems. Dishonest actions could occur at any stage of scientific research. Fabricated results may occur during data collection. Scientists can conduct legitimate tests but report results dishonestly by making up or altering them. Although both stages involve fabrication, falsification occurs only when dishonest actions take place. Misrepresentation of data occurs when data are collected and recorded honestly but are then represented in a dishonest manner. These occurrences are more ambiguous, such as the misuse of statistics in a written report or during court testimony. Dishonesty occurs with the intent to deceive, such as when people stretch the truth or lie when applying for grants. Additional examples of dishonesty in research include plagiarism and the misrepresentation of a scientist's publication status. *Plagiarism* is deceptive communication where someone misleads the audience by acting as if the words are their own. All examples of dishonest behavior are harmful to objective inquiry and public perception of science.

Publication in scientific journals is a crucial part of scientific research used to present technical information. Writing about research formalizes the results. Publication provides readers with the important facts and data without every minute detail. It is important to have awareness of the strengths and weaknesses of the work when communicating in a public forum. The information published on a given project should include data, materials, methods, names and institutional affiliation of authors, references, permission, acknowledgments, publication status, funding sources, and financial interests or conflicts of interests. Editors and reviewers should help authors improve on their work and treat authors with dignity and respect, should return manuscripts in a timely manner, and should help protect the confidentiality of manuscripts. These people are responsible for making fair, informed, and objective decisions regarding the publication. The peer review process creates a number of positive contributions to scientific publications. First, the process provides quality control. Peer review must be done carefully, critically, and objectively. Next, peer review involves privileged communication, assuring that the information is not copied or shared before publication. Finally, the findings are eventually made public for the purpose of broadening knowledge and expanding research. Publishing gives authors ownership and intellectual property over the research. Authorship is defined by the amount of responsibility and contribution to a project; if a person is willing to take credit, he or she must also take responsibility. Publishing provides scientists with the opportunity to share research findings, to advance knowledge, and to learn from the work of peers while maintaining open communication and the high standards of science.

There are occasions when publication might turn negative. Some journals may have goals that eliminate objectivity, which can highly damage a scientist's credibility. Also, there is pressure to publish because it enables scientists to secure grant funds, tenure, promotions, and professional prestige. Such pressure entices people to publish even if they are not the best qualified to do so. The pressure creates a rush to publish that can cause an increase in errors, biases, and deceptions. Selection of data for publication may create problems for researchers because, as the National Academy of Science states, "The selective use of research data is another area where the boundary between fabrication and creative insight may not be obvious (National Research Council, 2009)." Peer review is useful in determining what data can and should get omitted. Flaws found in the peer review process are typically due to a lack of time, desire, or funding for the reviewer to adequately accomplish his or her responsibility. One area that is increasingly problematic in the scientific community is the "least published unit," or the idea of publishing the same study in different forms. Publishing the same information repeatedly is not beneficial to science; it wastes resources and gives a person more recognition than he or she deserves. The final issue in scientific publication concerns awarding proper credit to contributors. Credit given through authorship when not deserved or by failing to recognize someone who made important contributions is a problem. Many scientists experience what Robert K. Merton coined the "Matthew effect," for the Gospel according to St. Matthew puts it this way:

> For unto every one that hath shall be given, and he shall have abundance: but from him that hath not shall be taken away even that which he hath.
>
> **Matthew 25:29**
> *King James Version*

The Matthew effect is more commonly known as the tendency for a noted scientist to get more credit than he or she deserves due to past accomplishments. When someone is considered an expert on a topic and he or she is the "second author," many colleagues may refer to the publication without mention of the true author. This tendency is fairly common in scientific publication—for example, when student interns conduct the majority of the work on a project while the mentor receives the majority of the recognition. Although publication is a useful tool in scientific research, it is important to avoid situations that may negatively impact the power of publication.

Ethics in Science and Research

Science is shaped by curiosity, conscience, and creativity—factors that are important in science and ethics because they contribute to new ideas, promote knowledge, and provide guidance. Creativity in science refers to finding truths and communicating facts, while general creativity is more involved with expression of thoughts and emotions. Ingenuity in science is comparable to puzzle solving; priorities are established, intricacies of main ideas are learned, values that conflict are merged with minor compromises, and new methods are developed as a result. The field of science has many challenges including the risk of failure, the lengthy process to reach a goal, hard work, doubt, funding, and the complexity and pressure of breaking new ground. Scientists are competitive, determined, and motivated by nature. Courage is necessary when creating new ideas, but does courage apply when the outcome is negative? For example, criminals are arguably courageous (in that what they do requires breaking societal norms and contains the implicit chance of being caught); however, is that the appropriate description since the outcome of their actions is bad? Science can provide facts that assist people in supporting or opposing moral arguments.

Though research entities strive for ethical practices, it is of common public opinion that research cannot be trusted. Due to this opinion, there is a prominent concern for the relationships among ethics, values, policy, and science. Scientists have a social responsibility to state the truth and the proper methods for conducting research in an ethical manner and should state the methods used as well. On one side are scientists who want to make a difference for others and may even risk their own lives to advance technology or knowledge. On the opposite side, some scientists turn away from work that conflicts with their own beliefs. Although compassion is a potential motive for science, it is not the primary motivation; many times the motivation is actually curiosity or some other self-serving reason. Good character, talent, luck, and nonmoral motives encourage the progress of science. The intellectual virtues of science include wisdom, truth, courage, humility, integrity, and self-respect. These factors contribute to accepted practices in science that are based on codes, standards, and laws determined as needed. For example, policies on data sharing exist because there is now a need for such standards. Scientists and trainees are responsible for refining existing standards, examining the subject, and developing new standards. Unfortunately, moral right and wrong does not always follow guidelines. At times it is difficult for a scientist to step back and assess issues objectively. In rare cases, scientists may sacrifice honesty and openness for social or political goals. Ethics are easier for scientists to identify with than morals because the latter often stem from instinct, feeling, environment, and faith whereas the former are based on rational analysis and professional duty. Scientists must have awareness of potential ethical dilemmas and how to avoid them to remain loyal to the values of science.

Professional ethics in science include good character, creativity, and responsibility in following a code of professional conduct. Though important, the standards of ethical conduct in science are more informal and ambiguous than in most other professions. The nature of science involves experimentation, communication, interpretation, and dissemination of ideas. Typically there is no standardized procedure in scientific investigation, which makes it difficult to create standards of conduct that encompass all potential issues. The main components of the moral ideal of science are the search for understanding scientific truths and open communication. The work of science is built on objectivity, honesty, tolerance, selflessness, and rationality of others. This foundation is then the basis for creation of more specific moral rules in science. Moral rules enable ethical decision making when problems arise. It is important to realize that scientific issues are composed of technical and ethical factors, although most scientists focus only on the technical side. Some decisions required of scientists include discarding data points, communicating work through scientific articles, and conducting proper laboratory practices to ensure safety. Scientific decisions have a technical side and an ethical side. To fully explore options, it is best to discuss the ethics of science in relation to actual situations and problems. Should society prohibit research for moral, political, or social reasons? Cloning is an example that is debated based on such reasons. What do you think? Do the potential benefits outweigh the potential harm? Can science fully participate in open communication while still protecting information? Does it make a difference if the investigation is in the early stages or late stages? If something has a potential ethical issue but is legitimate on the technical side, should the scientist continue on the project? These factors should be considered when studying the ethics of science and research.

Misconduct

Ethical issues could be general or specific to science. A study conducted in 2005 showed that one-third of scientists surveyed admitted to some sort of misconduct (Fanelli 2009). The most common forms of misconduct cited were a change in design, methods, or results in response to pressure from funding agencies, overlooked blemished data in past studies, having not followed proper procedure (e.g., consent of human subjects), and plagiarism or falsification of information.

First, scientists are urged to accelerate the transfer of knowledge into application and commercialization. This goal may produce an ethical issue such as *plagiarism*. The pressure to gain knowledge and spread it quickly may encourage scientists to use prior information without providing proper credit. Aside from obvious reasons not to plagiarize, published information has the ability to influence future research, professions, and policy. Next, there has been an increase in the abuse of peer review. Some concerns include delay of publications of competitors or those with similar research, reviewers who are not critical enough of works because they favor the methods used, and reviewers who are overly critical of works that support something they oppose. In addition, journals are now asking authors and reviewers for financial interest reports to assure that there are no conflicts of interest. For example, Harry Snyder Jr. and Renee Peugeot Snyder forged clinical trial data to support a lymphoma and psoriasis treatment. This earned them company stock and options worth more than $600,000 while working for the company that conducted the study (Grant 2009). Finally, funding in general may create problems for scientists. It is important for scientists to consider potential conflicts of interest with funding sources, although in response to some issues, grant review panels and advisory boards have established conflict of interest guidelines. Scientists must assure that their work is not compromised due to funding sources, such as managing information in ways dictated by those funding the work or falsifying data to obtain additional funding.

The top two funding agencies of fundamental science are the National Institutes of Health (NIH) and the National Science Foundation (NSF). NIH is an agency of the Department of Health and Human Safety (DHHS), which has recently expanded the scientific integrity department. The DHHS definition of misconduct excludes breaking the law as scientific misconduct; rather, it is seen as violations of law, such as embezzling grant funds, vandalizing equipment, and sexual harassment. The definition also states that scientists might disagree about the interpretation of results and could make errors that are not scientific misconduct, accounting for the human factor of science. NSF's definition of misconduct states that if an action does harm to science, it should be considered scientific misconduct. Both agencies have strict rules forbidding fabrication, falsification, and plagiarism. In 1993, the NIH Revitalization Act established the Commission on Research Integrity (CRI). The sole purpose of the commission was to create a universal definition of scientific misconduct.

Funding is a large part of conducting scientific research and creates the potential for misconduct. Government funding for research is minimal, which is why outside funding is sought for scientific research. In fact, 75% of funding for clinical trials comes from corporate sponsors. Objectivity is difficult because of potential conflicts between the researcher and funding agency. For instance, funding agencies can modify the content, scope, and definitions of research to fit certain political agendas rather than the objective criteria set forth by a scientist. If the researcher speaks out against such actions, he or she runs the risk of having the research funding stopped. On the other hand, ethically the research may not intend to receive funding with an organization that has such control over the research. Aside from the issues of control, researchers may need to refrain from seeking funding from certain agencies if there is a conflict of interest. If conflicts are possible, the researcher should disclose information regarding the relationship before research begins. Currently, there is no correlation between economic conflicts of interest and the prevalence of falsification, fabrication, or plagiarism. In fact, it is hypothesized that the economic ties to business may actually prevent fabrication and falsification of data because people are much more cautious to avoid issues.

A potential area for misconduct in science is record keeping. Although it is often learned passively, there is a basis for good record keeping. Good records are legible and organized, allow for reproducibility, and are complete concerning the scientific contribution. Information regarding experiments should contain a purpose statement, materials used, methods, observations, results, discussion, and data pages, if necessary. In addition, scientists should include why and how particular steps were taken, what did and did not happen throughout the experiment, the interpretation of results, and, if applicable, the steps necessary to follow up. The records should foster accuracy and reliability for reproducibility. The information provided in records is considered data when it has authenticity, integrity, and can be used for logical reasoning. Record keeping is less likely to promote misconduct if guidelines and training on proper procedures are provided. Laboratory leaders should develop policies that include a statement on data ownership and retention. It is common for organizations to have a particular way of recording data; scientists should comply with their agencies' requirements concerning reports and data.

Data management is an important area of scientific research that requires integrity. Managing data is not a problem if it is organized with a high-quality system. The ideal system enables scientists to check their own work, critics and reviewers to scrutinize or verify research, and other scientists to use the provided data. Although a piece of data is not significant in one study, it may have value to another so it is not completely unnecessary. Access granted to collaborators, colleagues, other scientists, and representatives from funding agencies is useful. Sometimes scientists may have an obligation to destroy data after a certain amount of time. In addition to having a time limitation, some researchers may intentionally limit who has access to the data. There are many reasons for prevention; for example, nonexperts could accidentally destroy it, rivals could steal it, enemies could intentionally destroy it, or other people could misinterpret what is presented in the data. Political reasons also influence researchers to selectively release data. Though limiting certain persons may seem to go against the openness of science, it prevents potential destruction of the data to keep the information "safe." Science is a profession that maintains checks and balances to ensure accuracy.

Ethics in Forensic Science

5

> The temptation for the forensic scientist ... is to become a servant of the police and the criminal prosecutor's office to the extent that truth is sacrificed .... Such forensic scientists improperly join in the chase for a likely suspect and resolve doubts in support of their colleagues in the police department.
>
> **William Curran**

Introduction

Forensic science is a historical science applied to criminal investigation and legal matters. The goal of investigation is to determine what crime was committed, who committed the crime, and what evidence is pertinent to the crime. *Evidence* is anything that helps prove or disprove material facts. The goal of forensic scientists is to examine evidence and to convey the results to investigators and attorneys via reports and testimony. Criminal investigation involves police, attorneys, and scientists. It is the job of the police officers, detectives, or crime scene investigators to report to the scene of a crime. Once the scene is processed, forensic scientists analyze the evidence that crime scene personnel have recovered. Forensic scientist positions used to primarily consist of trained biologists or chemists who received on-the-job training and gained experience for the legal aspects of the job. Within the last 20 years, graduate and undergraduate programs in forensic science have become the norm. Since the O. J. Simpson trial, the public has become increasingly aware of the value of forensic analysis. With the increased popularity have come a number of television shows depicting Hollywood's version of forensic science. Although glamorous and fast-paced, the media depicts a deceiving reality of forensic science. The public is led to believe that important evidence is found in every crime, that cases are always solved and quickly, and that, with the aid of technology, instruments do the work for the scientists. The true value of scientist is also skewed by the Hollywood characters' ability to carry guns, to question witnesses, to process crime scenes, and to analyze a variety of evidence when, in reality, such a job is conducted by many people (and unless a sworn officer, the person does not get to carry a gun). The issues mentioned may facilitate unethical behavior if a scientist allows such hype to become a distraction or an influence. This chapter looks at the reality of forensic science.

Crime Scene

Forensic science begins at the scene of a crime. Once the commission of a crime occurs, police officers and, if applicable, crime scene investigators or technicians report to the scene. Their job is to document, collect, and preserve evidence for analysis. The standard operating procedures and protocols for processing a crime scene may vary between agencies and jurisdictions but include documentation, collection, transportation, and submission of evidence to the crime laboratory. Although protocols and procedures are in place, every scene is unique. As variables are encountered, investigators must use the individual situation as their guide. Important qualities investigators should possess include flexibility, improvisation, and creativity.

Visual documentation is important before crime scene processing begins. Such documentation occurs with the use of photography and videography to capture a crime scene. Victims, potential evidence, and the surroundings are shown in detail, which allows for a complete review after the scene has been processed. As technology has increased with the use of digital media, so has the chance for deception. Although digital media provides stable, long-term storage of images, forensic scientists are beginning to question the source and authenticity of some digital image data. Changes to images are so easy to make that altered images may be returned to analog format and used to replace the original image. So what safeguards may forensic scientists use to assure that images remain reliable and acceptable forms of evidence? First, scientists should view images in the context of the case. Next, the source of the image and the chain of custody must be considered. Finally, the importance of the image to the case needs to be weighed: Is it a key piece of evidence? Would someone try to alter it? The digital media issue has increased the awareness of a need for the adaption of standards for all forensic imaging.

Communication is crucial for assuring that everyone knows his or her role in processing the scene. Written communication is essential to assure that laboratory personnel get a clear picture of the crime scene and evidence as it was discovered, without having been present. Notes and sketches that are thorough, complete, and descriptive are useful. Many forensic scientists will tell you that if it is not written, it did not happen. This serves everyone's interest because the process of forensic science and law occur slowly. A case may not go to court until years after the crime occurred. Not only does the initial documentation help investigators piece evidence together, but it also serves as a reminder to scientists of what happened, who was responsible for the parts of the analysis, how things were done, and what the results showed.

Notes should also provide the context of evidence because this may determine how the evidence is processed, collected, and later analyzed. For example, blood that is pooled around a victim's body clearly demonstrates that the source of the blood is the victim. This information would serve investigators to understand the situation of the crime but also to establish how the evidence should be processed. In this example, bloodstain pattern analysis would be more useful than sampling the blood for DNA analysis. In all cases, it is important to collect questioned and known samples of evidence such as hairs, fibers, blood, fingerprints, paint, soil, glass, and handwriting. Samples with a known original origin are *known samples*. When the original source is unknown, the samples are considered *questioned*. Crime scene examination is a crucial step in the investigative process where people collect and preserve evidence that could alter the course of someone's life. Even simple mistakes can damage an entire investigation, so it is important for those at the crime scene to take their time, to act methodically, to document all information, and to maintain the integrity of the evidence before presenting the evidence to the crime laboratory.

Laboratory

Meaningful work, like a meaningful life, is morally worthy work undertaken in a morally worthy organization. Work has meaning *because* there is some good in it … Work makes life better if it helps others; alleviates suffering; eliminates difficult, dangerous, or tedious toil, makes someone healthier and happier; or aesthetically or intellectually enriches people and improves the environment in which we live.

Joanne B. Ciulla

Crime laboratories, which have historically started as departments within law enforcement agencies or as basic scientific laboratories, are responsible for analyzing evidence resulting from the commission of crimes. Crime laboratories are either in the public or private sector. Most crime laboratories in the United States are considered public; that is, they are operated by the federal, state, or local government. Private laboratories typically specialize in a few types of evidence, are for-profit entities, and will primarily accept cases from law enforcement officials when requested. Although the majority of private laboratories do not accept evidence or cases from accused persons directly, some will. Each state has at least one crime laboratory, and, as with most parts of forensic science, there is no set structure. The internal organization and services offered varies by jurisdiction, agency, personnel, size, location, budget, and crime statistics of the area where the laboratory is located. The differences between agencies do not impact the actual science of investigation.

Investigators submit evidence to the laboratory with clearly documented information so scientists can best decide on the analyses to conduct. The information includes what evidence is submitted, what criminal circumstances surround the crime, which investigator is submitting the items, and what examinations are requested of the laboratory. Evidence may have varying levels of importance depending on the circumstances of the crime and crime scene so it is helpful when investigators provide such information to the laboratory. The investigator must account for details such as the relationships among people, places, and things involved in crime because these details are important to determine what examinations scientists will perform. For example, an attack by a stranger will give more relative evidence than an attack by a person's spouse. In addition to the information provided when submitting evidence to a crime laboratory, there are protocols for the order in which sections of the laboratory should receive evidence (if multiple examinations are necessary). Some forms of evidence are more resilient than others and withstand multiple forms of analysis without getting destroyed in the process. The two processes involved in evidence analysis are identification and comparison. Identification is when a scientist recognizes and states what something is. Comparison is the examination of like materials to determine if they have a common source and, if a common one is found, to determine what that source is. Analysis allows scientists to determine facts regarding the evidence.

Science is repeatable and testable, thus making it a useful part of criminal investigations. *Controls*, or materials whose source is known and are used for comparison with unknown evidence, are important in forensic science. There are two types of controls: positive and negative. *Positive controls* occur when a test is run on a sample and the test yields a positive or expected result. *Negative controls* occur when tests are run on a sample that is known not to be a particular substance and the result is negative. Why are controls important? Controls assure that the science is working. If scientists do not run negative controls, *false positives* could occur; they describe a positive result for something that is not correct. An example is when a test confirms the presence of blood, even if the substance is not blood. False positives cause Type I errors in which innocent people are falsely incriminated. On the other hand, if scientists do not run positive controls, it could lead to *false negatives* or a conclusion that a bloodstain is something other than blood. Such conclusions cause Type II errors in which people are falsely exonerated from a crime they actually committed. Of these errors, a Type I error is much worse than a Type II error because the law would rather someone be wrongly set free than wrongly imprisoned (Houck and Siegel 2006). Testability is a hallmark of science; however, scientists must understand the limitations imposed on this feature. It is important for scientists to familiarize themselves with the methods and procedures of the science to properly present information regarding the evidence to the triers-of-fact. Laboratory results vary in format but should consistently include facts such as the name, agency, and contact information for the examiner; the methods used for analysis; the case number and date; the items examined; the results determined; and any relevant statistics. As the destination of forensic investigation is typically the courtroom, scientists should remember that reports are mostly written for officers, attorneys, and judges so the reports should be complete, concise summaries void of overly technical information.

There are many potential ethical issues to consider regarding evidence; however, the most important step to avoid problems is to present relevant evidence. Scientists must examine all relevant evidence and ensure that samples are not completely consumed or altered without correct documentation. Chain of custody is imperative for court—the documentation that tracks evidence each time it changes hands or is moved between locations. In court, the value or "weight" of evidence typically depends on the type and quality of the evidence. No matter what the evidence, forensic scientists must obtain information in a way that satisfies the scientific requirements of validity, reliability, accuracy, and precision. Forensic scientists are not advocates for anyone; they must remain impartial and report the findings based on science. It is helpful to provide the jury with demonstrative evidence in court. Demonstrative evidence does not occur directly from the crime itself but is a result of the investigation such as photos, sketches, or testimony. Demonstrative evidence peaks jurors' interest, regains jurors' attention, reemphasizes key points, and supports the judges and jurors' memory of evidence. It is also useful in providing the visual learner with a clearer idea of the topic or evidence. Finally, demonstrative evidence allows experts to assume a more authoritative appearance for the triers-of-fact. It is at this point where scientists must know not only the details of the science they conduct and the reasons for analyses but also the rules of conduct that govern their testifying as an expert witness at some point in their career.

Role of the Scientific Expert Witness

Court testimony may be required of anyone involved in the investigative process. Expert witnesses are used to provide relevant information from their specific role in the investigation, have more knowledge on a subject than the average person, and are able to provide the court with opinions. The triers-of-fact then determine guilt or innocence based on a variety of evidence. Evidence is information provided through testimony, materials, or documentation. So what exactly is an *expert* witness? An expert witness, according to Federal Rule of Evidence 702, is "one who by reason of education or specialized experience possesses superior knowledge respecting a subject about which persons having no particular training are incapable of forming an accurate opinion or deducing a correct conclusion" (Fed. R. Evid. 702 (1988)). Knowledge and expertise on a particular case (i.e., officers, detectives, and crime scene personnel) or on specific evidence (i.e., lab scientist) constitutes a forensic scientist as the *expert*. Law has defined the role of an expert as an impartial educator who assists the triers-of-fact by providing specialized knowledge to help decide the outcome of a case. The expert is also an instrument of the attorney and court, making that person a *witness*. Forensic experts are used to provide scientific and technical information within their area of expertise to judges and juries. Experts have an ethical obligation to define their area and level of expertise and should not testify beyond that level of expertise. Expert testimony is based on facts and honesty. Expert witnesses should provide a simple statement of their education, an evaluation of the relevant evidence, and a presentation of their findings in court. Experts must be willing to volunteer information that may be ethically, though not legally, required. In addition, experts must point out the nature of scientific findings and acknowledge contradictory evidence when it exists. Scientists have an ethical obligation to inform the attorneys of the limitations of the scientific evidence. Juries tend to give a disproportionate amount of weight to expert testimony, so experts should not abuse the authority they have in the courtroom. Experts hold a position in the gray area of working in a court of law while exhibiting nonlegal expertise.

> Academics and the legal system do not usually co-exist in comfort. The laws of science and the rules of evidence have little in common. In theory, Academia functions on the principle of collegiality. In theory and reality, the American legal system is adversarial. The average academic entering the legal system is in for a tremendous culture shock. (Goff 2000, p. 5)[*]

It has been said that scientists should enter a courtroom and accommodate the law. This perception may be interpreted in a number of ways. First, is this statement implying that scientists should act unethically if that is the precedent set by the court? Next, is the statement implying that experts are brought into the court as pawns of the attorneys? Finally, is the statement specifically referring to the scientists' testimony, demeanor, or scientific nature? Alan Goldman states that scientists should "accept limitations on their authority to act on direct moral perception...." However, it has also been stated that "if the law has made you a witness, remain a man of science; you have no victim to avenge, no guilty or innocent person to ruin or save. You must bear testimony within the limits of science" (Saviers 2002, p. 460).

---

[*] Goff, L. 2000. *A Fly for the Prosecution: How Insect Evidence Helps Solve Crimes.* Cambridge, MA: Harvard University Press.

When scientists enter court, they must be careful in what they say and how they say it. It is the job of those in the adversarial system to discredit the experts' testimony and, at times, even the experts themselves. Jurors should exhibit caution and not overweigh evidence and information provided by experts.

Though expert witnesses do not have formal rules for testifying, there are some common informal rules to follow. Experts should not discuss the case with anyone outside of court. One may not know the suspects, victims, family members, or opposing council, so it is best not to risk providing information that could negatively impact the trial. Experts should avoid advocacy and defensive or argumentative responses. These actions may feel natural when conducting business in the adversarial system; however, by preventing natural instincts the experts will reinforce their credibility with the court and the triers-of-fact. Expert witnesses should immediately stop talking if the judge or attorney interrupts. If yes–no questions need clarification, the experts should request permission to answer in greater detail than the original question required. Experts cannot avoid questions if they believe the answer will support the opposing side; the worst thing forensic experts do for their credibility is to show bias or hesitate to give an objective answer. Written reports should be thorough, concise, readable, and objective; should not fail to provide requested details; may contain reviews of relevant literature, statistics, and resources used; and finally should present an opportunity for the expert to provide all necessary information without the common interruptions that occur in a courtroom. Reports should also include information regarding work conducted by anyone else other than the expert. Experts should not volunteer information without being asked, should not guess answers, and should not generalize. The experts' testimony is less effective when it is presented in a generalized manner, although some attorneys may push the experts into such a method of response. An ethical dilemma is created as a result and should be avoided as much as possible. It is acceptable, and at times expected, that experts will respond to questions with the answer, "I do not know"; qualification as an expert does not make someone an expert on all topics. Expert testimony may cite the opinions of authors and base answers off standard information found in scientific books and journals. Experts should assure that they fully understand questions before answering, recognize the weaknesses of their opinions, and prepare for questions regarding those possible weaknesses. Examples of "weak" opinions include those based on prior testimony in the case where new technologies or methods have developed since the previous testimony. The most important "rule" for ethical expert witnesses is to present opinions truthfully after all information is collected and examinations are completed. These are just some of the informal rules that prepare a scientist to present expert testimony for the judicial system.

Expert witness testimony may have a significant impact on juries because it is considered highly credible. It is important that the information provided by experts measure up to the jury's expectations of reliability. Scientists should avoid "junk science," evidence that is not consistent with generally accepted scientific views. Daubert criteria have helped to eliminate this issue in court and are discussed further in upcoming sections. Experts receive criticism if their testimony is speculative, includes facts not deemed from the evidence, is not relevant, is common knowledge, or is based on inadmissible information. The jury may have difficulty processing evidence when both the prosecution and defense have experts. Conflicting testimony by two expert witnesses happens; it may occur because the focus is on different measures, interpretations vary, the experts use different approaches, or the scientists were trained in different schools of thought. Even if expert opinions conflict, it does not necessarily make one more right or wrong. It is possible that both points are valid based on specific research. Literature serves as a guide, but in the truth of science, facts are meant to be challenged. Science is ever changing, which is how uncertainty in science becomes an obstacle for expert witnesses. The adversary process does not allow for the exchange of information between experts when facts conflict, which is needed to help overcome uncertainty. If witnesses could communicate with the opposing expert, they may receive clarity regarding the origin of their differences in opinion. Additional drawbacks for the expert witnesses include the risk of damage to their reputation if the opposing council discredits them, contradictory information provided by opposing experts that may make science look divided and unreliable, fees charged by private experts that encourage bias (or the perception of bias), and the lack of fees for public experts that may create problems of witnesses undermining information. Other issues aside, providing expert testimony comes with a great responsibility to the scientist and to the jury. Expert witnesses are held in high esteem by the jury, so it is important to provide information accurately and authoritatively.

Qualification

How does one *become* an expert witness? First, a scientist must undergo a process where a judge qualifies them as an expert, also known as *voir dire*. It is during this process that a person's knowledge, skills, experience, education, and training are established for a judge. The amount of experience required differs based on the judge, the court, and the topic of expertise. Second, expert opinions must be based on reliable information such as journals, reports, texts, or personal experience. Next, the knowledge that the expert is providing must assist the triers-of-fact in understanding the subject matter. Finally, expert testimony must relate to information beyond common experience and knowledge. Once an expert is qualified, judges must determine if expert testimony is relevant to the case based on the Federal Rules of Evidence. Regarding expert testimony, Rule 702 of the Federal Rules of Evidence states, "If scientific, technical, or other specialized knowledge will assist the triers-of-fact to understand the evidence or to determine a fact in issue, a witness qualified as an expert … may testify thereto in the form of an opinion or otherwise" (Fed. R. Evid. 702 [1988]).

It is important for the expert witnesses to exemplify the role of *reporter of facts*, not *advocate* for one side or another. One should remember that experts are human, so mistakes can and will happen; however, mistakes need to occur as infrequently as possible. Expert witnesses must also have awareness of the perceived weaknesses in their testimony; this may include problems with the training or education, the science, the methods used, or the actual evidence. In addition to these weaknesses, experts must realize that the manner in which they are retained could be used to challenge their testimony. Experts may act as testifying expert witnesses or private consultants. Private experts are sought for their reputation and expertise and for their ability to analyze and explain the complexities of the science in simple terms for the legal purpose, to present opinions understandably and "holes" in the opinions of the opposing theory. In addition, consulting expert witnesses are selected based on their work habits, attitude, and personality (e.g., Do they easily get along with others?). Potential biases and potential conflicts of interest are facts to consider for attorneys hiring scientific experts. Though an expert is affiliated with a state or local agency, it does not mean that he or she will never act in the role of private expert. Many scientists keep working in the consultant capacity after retirement.

Court-hired experts (and procedures to do such) support high levels of ethics and competency because in this case experts are evaluated and chosen based on objectivity. In the case of court-hired experts, financial incentives would favor a neutral third party, such as the judge, not the prosecutor or defense. Expert testimony is important in the judicial system because it provides reliable scientific knowledge and relevant information to assist the triers-of-fact.

Once the experts are qualified as such based on credentials, they need to present information and evidence to the triers-of-fact. It is important that experts present themselves and the evidence appropriately. Experts are teachers; they simplify and explain complex ideas and terms simply, translate technical language into lay terms, and provide the triers-of-fact with assistance in the comprehension of scientific and technical issues. Experts are communicators who offer evidence in a clear, confident, and concise manner. Personal characteristics that support experts' success are self-confidence, honesty, competitiveness, and leadership. If experts command a room with a quiet confidence, avoid exaggeration and aggression, and gain trust quickly, they are considered excellent witnesses. Testimony that is presented in a clear, concise, and understandable manner with eye contact and proper body language is the goal. Experts should avoid arrogance, argumentative responses, and negativity toward the opposing expert or attorney. Although providing expert testimony is not an exact science, some learned behaviors make testifying less stressful for experts. Proper public speaking that uses inflection, pauses, gestures, volume and does not become monotone is useful in court. Before testifying, experts should have a general understanding of how their area of expertise is pertinent to the case. Experts should prepare for court by reviewing the relevant science, terminology, and standards. Pretrial conferences between the scientist and the attorneys are valuable means of preparation. These meetings help the expert to provide information to the attorneys about what the evidence did and did not show. It also allows the expert to better explain the science to assist the attorney in preparation for his or her questioning. Such meetings provide the expert with insight on the attorney's style of questioning. Although not mandatory, pretrial conferences between the attorney and expert benefit both parties in the courtroom. The expert may also prepare for court by reviewing written reports, notes, and case facts. While testifying, it is important that the expert speak directly to the jury to assist the expert in determining what information is understood and what needs clarification. When answering questions, experts should avoid hearsay, refer to notes only when necessary, have awareness of prior statements given, and answer only what is asked. Attorneys may word questions in a confusing manner to mislead the expert, so it is imperative that the expert listen carefully and take caution with multicomponent questions. If the expert realizes he or she has been misled, the expert should not become argumentative; it is the expert's duty to remain calm and composed to positively represent the field and the science. Personal characteristics and some learned behaviors assist the expert in successfully conveying scientific information in court.

Admissibility of Scientific Evidence

Only admissible evidence is used in court proceedings, but what *determines* admissibility? Admissibility of evidence is regulated by the Federal Rules of Evidence. These rules were developed in 1973 and govern the introduction of evidence in civil and criminal proceedings. The Federal Rules of Evidence incorporate the judge-made decisions and common evidentiary rules that were in effect at the time of their adoption. If the Federal Rules contain gaps or omissions, courts may answer questions by relying on precedent. The factors that deem evidence inadmissible include prejudice, unreliability, and privilege. Evidence that causes prejudice includes anything that could turn the triers-of-fact against the accused. Examples of prejudicial evidence include graphic images of a victim presented by color photographs or facts that highlight a prior incident, not for which the accused is currently being tried. Unreliable evidence includes eyewitness testimony, hearsay, or evidence that has not gone through the process of discovery. Privilege could affect the admissibility of evidence because in cases of attorney–client or doctor–patient privilege, protection is offered from having to offer testimony on persons or information that is considered confidential.

> Federal Rule 702, "*Testimony by Experts*," says, "If scientific, technical, or other specialized knowledge will assist the triers-of-fact to understand the evidence or to determine a fact in issue, a witness qualified as an expert by knowledge, skill, experience, training, or education, may testify thereto in the form of an opinion or otherwise, if (1) the testimony is based upon sufficient facts or data, (2) the testimony is the product of reliable principles and methods, and (3) the witness has applied the principles and methods reliably to the facts of the case" (Fed. R. Evid. 702 (1988)).

The *Frye* Case

Frye v. United States (54 App. D.C. 46, 47, 293 F. 1013, 1014 [1923]) is a landmark Supreme Court decision that involved the admissibility of scientific evidence. This was a criminal case that entailed the results of a systolic blood pressure test, commonly known as a polygraph, in a murder trial. At the time, the test was seen as a novel technique, and the court decided that the evidence was not admissible based on the fact that it was not generally accepted by the relevant scientific community. The evidence presented therefore was not generally accepted and not admitted. It was then determined that as scientific evidence advances from experimental to demonstrable, the principles behind the science receive general acceptance from the professional community or field before considered admissible by the courts. This standard was established and became known as the *Frye* test of general acceptance. The following statement from *Frye v. United States* (1923) has become known as the *Frye* rule or test of general acceptance:

> Just when a scientific principle or discovery crosses the line between the experimental and demonstrable stages is difficult to define. Somewhere in this twilight zone the evidential force of the principle must be recognized, and while courts will go a long way in admitting expert testimony deduced from a well-recognized scientific principle or discovery, the thing from which the deduction is made must be sufficiently established to have gained general acceptance in the particular field in which it belongs.

The *Frye* rule is the expert's opinion based on what is *generally accepted* by the scientific community. The specifics are unclear, but time has shown that the primary criterion is that the science has been published in a peer-reviewed journal—although exceptions do exist. A potential problem for scientists is the law dictating what is regarded as scientific evidence. Lawyers and judges dictate what constitutes scientific evidence (Bowen 2006). The *Frye* rule is only one example of the admissibility of scientific evidence. Currently the United States has an even distribution of states adhering to the *Frye* rule and states adhering to the Daubert standards.

The Daubert Case

Daubert v. Merrell-Dow Pharmaceuticals, Inc. ([92-102], 509 U.S. 579 [1993]) was a U.S. Supreme Court case that involved a morning sickness pill. The drug was produced by Merrell-Dow Pharmaceuticals and was alleged to cause birth defects. The plaintiffs in *Daubert* were the parents of children born with the birth defects; the women took the drug Bendectin while they were pregnant to reduce morning sickness. Merrell-Dow contended that Bendectin did not cause birth defects and presented an expert in birth defect epidemiology for the defense. The expert claimed that he had reviewed all of the relevant literature and found no evidence to prove that Bendectin caused birth defects. The plaintiffs offered eight different experts to conclude that Bendectin did cause birth defects, based on animal cell studies, life animal studies, and chemical structure analysis. The District Court agreed with Merrell-Dow Pharmaceuticals and concluded that the plaintiff's opposing expert opinions were not admissible because the methodology was not sufficiently established to have general acceptance in the field. The U.S. Court of Appeals for the Ninth Circuit affirmed the District Court's ruling because the plaintiff's evidence was generated only to use in court rather than being based on peer-reviewed and published scientific knowledge (*Daubert v. Merrell-Dow Pharmaceuticals, Inc.*, 951 F. 2d 1128 [9th Cir. 1991]).

The *Daubert* standard deals with the admissibility of expert witness testimony during legal proceedings. The testimony of the expert must be both relevant and reliable. Within Daubert, relevancy means that the expert's theory or opinion has to fit the facts of the case. Even if the expert's theory is completely scientific, it has no relevance if the theory deals with a matter that was not an issue in the case. Reliability is deemed when the expert derives his or her conclusions by a scientific method. In 1993, the Supreme Court issued its first ruling on the admissibility of scientific evidence. *Daubert v. Merrell-Dow Pharmaceuticals* provided five factors that should be considered by the trial judges when determining whether expert opinion testimony is scientifically valid and reliable:

1. The theory or technique must be *falsifiable, refutable,* and *testable.*
2. The theory or technique has been subjected to *peer review* and *publication*. The court stated that "submission to the scrutiny of

the scientific community is a component of 'good science,' in part because it increases the likelihood that substantive flaws in methodology will be detected."

3. *Known or potential error rates* of the theory or technique should be considered.

4. The existence and maintenance of *standards* and controls for the theory or technique.

5. Whether the theory and technique is *generally accepted* by a relevant scientific community and has a bearing on the inquiry. This factor uses the initial criteria set forth by the Frye case while expanding on it.

The Supreme Court emphasized that these factors do not constitute a checklist and that the inquiry must remain flexible. The Daubert case has allowed the trial judges to act as "gatekeepers." The judges are able to decide whether to permit experts to present expert evidence to a jury. This issue poses difficulties for scientists because when judges have the gatekeeper role, differing results between courtrooms may occur. What one courtroom may deem admissible, another may reject. Despite potential issues, this case changed the rules of the standards of evidence admissibility. The Daubert case has also recently caused many forensic science disciplines to reevaluate the amount of demonstrated scientific research on topics. Among those disciplines are fingerprint examiners, document examiners, and hair examiners. Today, *Daubert* is the leading U.S. Supreme Court case regarding the admissibility of expert witness opinion as evidence in the federal courts (Daubert v. Merrell-Dow Pharmaceuticals, 509, U.S. 579, 1993).

Parameters

There is an expectation that the forensic expert will be ethical in examining and evaluating evidence, in reporting data, in presenting opinions, and in dealing with the relevant people (attorneys, plaintiffs, defendants, judges, and juries). What is considered "ethical behavior" is a vague concept because there are no specific conduct rules for forensic scientists within the law. Most forensic scientists are not specifically trained in testimony or the rules of litigation, including the ethics of law. Training is needed to prepare scientists as expert witnesses. Necessary education is obtained by courses, seminars, workshops, and publications. In addition to training on the scientific perspective, an increase in publication by attorneys regarding how to "deal" with expert witnesses would be helpful. Attorneys could provide experts with insight into the judicial side of expert testimony by preparing the expert with information on specialized examinations, general advice, and courtroom briefings. Scientific professional organizations typically have professional codes of conduct for members that provide ethical standards for the expert witness. In addition, experts are regulated by state and federal rules, laws, and court decisions.

One area of concern, though typically more of an issue with private experts, is fees for service. Fees are allowable for expert witnesses as long as the details are decided on before the expert is retained for their services and openly communicated to the court. Experts should estimate the time needed for each case so attorneys have a clear idea of the total cost; if the case takes longer than expected and causes an increase in fees, experts should notify the attorney of the new cost. Customary fees are decided by factors such as the field, the specialty area, and the expert's experience and reputation. Courts have a right to lower the fee if not considered "reasonable." When experts set high fees to discourage attorneys from retaining their service, it looks very bad for the experts when they are called to testify. It is considered unethical for forensic experts to pay for case referrals, although they may pay a service to list their contact information on a directory of experts. Advertising is not unethical but should occur in a professional manner as to not create problems if brought up in testimony. An example is an attorney stating that an expert "is in the business of testifying," which can tarnish the expert's credibility.

Another area of ethical concern stems from contingency fees, which are outcome based. In such cases, opinions are more likely seen as biased. To help guide the discussion of fees and eliminate potential misconduct, the National Forensic Center has a guide for expert witness fees. Although the law does not regulate expert conduct, there are some policies in place to encourage appropriate behavior. Though some experts feel their testimony is more valuable and has more weight than other evidence, experts are simply a means for an attorney to facilitate the jury's understanding. It is important to remember that law makes one an expert witness, but the person must also remain true to science. As Peter DeForest states, *"There is a need to recognize the difference between the 'opinion of a scientist' and a 'scientific opinion.' The former may have no scientific basis and, if so, is out of place in any scientific report or testimony"* (Bowen 2006, 3-3).

There is a focus on the problems associated with expert testimony. The first problem is the legacy imposed on an expert by his or her predecessors or the legacy of the agency in which the expert is employed. Professional organizations sustain a community of experts and must assure that their members behave responsibly to prevent issues. Next, the lack of specific forensic training for expert witnesses within their disciplines has brought about concern. This concern tends to include the variation of qualifications, certifications, and training among experts. In addition, there are great pressures on the experts from many sources, as we have discussed to this point. Finally, the conflicts of interest imposed by the judicial system pose problems for the scientific experts. The judicial system should take some actions to avoid suffering the consequences of calling an expert witness. Such actions include protecting experts from the effects of advocacy, developing validation procedures to evaluate testimony, and establishing criteria to identify "experts." Although potential problems surround the use of expert witnesses, they are minor in comparison with the value of having expert testimony. Identifying problems regarding expert testimony is the first step toward resolution.

Misconduct

Crime laboratories face high demands, large workloads, minimal budgets, and extensive backlogs all under the scrutiny of the public. Misconduct occurs by agencies as a whole just as it occurs by individuals. Areas of concern for the scientist where ethical dilemmas could most easily occur include chain of custody, turnaround time for testing, preservation and sampling of evidence, and provision of adequate reports. Sources of pressure that may lead to ethical misconduct vary. First, it is not mandatory for forensic laboratories to seek accreditation. Currently there is an elective mechanism in place set forth by the American Society of Crime Laboratory Directors-Laboratory Accreditation Board (ASCLD-LAB). Many states are requiring laboratories to seek accreditation, and many of the states not required to seek accreditation still aspire to meet the criteria of accreditation. Another issue regarding accreditation is that the process endorses the laboratory itself, not the individual scientists. The American Society for Testing and Materials (ASTM) E30 standards for forensic science are voluntary standards to assist in accreditation of agencies. Another source of pressure that influences a scientist's experience in court is access to the laboratory and its resources. Laboratories typically support a parent agency, customarily a law enforcement agency. This means that police officers, detectives, crime scene personnel, and prosecutors have access to laboratory services, while defense attorneys do not have the same resources (free laboratory services) available to them. The imbalance caused by this access may provide an additional source of pressure for the forensic scientist, although it is beyond the scientist's control.

Conflicts and frustrations among forensic scientists occur because of the law enforcement culture, the adversary system, rules of science and from within individuals. A common problem for forensic laboratories is that some are expected to function according to the mandates of their consumers, which is often the law enforcement community or lawyers. It is not easy to determine which ethics to follow when involved with more than one profession. These relationships can create pressure to expand the area of ethical conduct and can have some serious consequences. First, tasks assigned to scientists by supervisors might reflect priorities set by the prosecutor's office or the police department, whichever is the governing organization. Funding allocation to the laboratories may also be affected by the governing organization. Next, the pursuit of criminal convictions along with selective consideration of evidence may determine what information or evidence is provided to scientists to evaluate, and this is typically beyond the scientists' control. Finally, the law enforcement agency that houses a laboratory can control rewards and sanctions for the forensic scientists. Additional pressure stems from the conflicting ethics of science and law enforcement cultures. Scientists are expected to find the "right" answer for tests, and typically police officers think the right answer is the one that points toward guilt of the defendant. Science is supportive in the criminal justice system, so one would expect such pressures and expectations were not an issue. Scientists must have control over their work and convince others in the criminal justice system that objectivity is of the utmost importance. Forensic scientists with a good sense of personal and professional ethics will avoid dilemmas no matter how great the differences are in the professional cultures. These are some of the issues forensic scientists may face when dealing with the conflicting goals of scientific laboratories and law enforcement.

Barry Fisher's (2000) *Techniques of Crime Scene Investigation* includes a list of ethical misconduct specific to forensic science:

- Planting evidence at a crime scene to point to a defendant.
- Collecting evidence without a warrant by claiming exigent circumstances.
- Falsifying laboratory examinations to enhance the prosecutor's case.
- Ignoring evidence at a crime scene that might exonerate a suspect or be a mitigating factor.
- Reporting on forensic tests not actually done out of a misguided belief that the tests are unnecessary.
- Fabricating scientific opinions based on invalid interpretations of tests or evidence to assist the prosecution.
- Examining physical evidence when not qualified to do so.
- Extending expertise beyond one's knowledge.
- Using unproved methodologies.
- Overstating an expert opinion by using "terms of art" unfamiliar to juries.
- Failing to report a colleague, superior, or subordinate who engages in any of the previously listed activities to the proper authorities.

Forensic scientists are in high-pressure positions. Power and influence accompany the professional privilege of public trust. This power and influence is why some courts are against expert testimony. Professional privilege of forensic scientists is a common misconception of the layperson as a result of the "CSI effect." Some lawyers and judges feel that jurors educated about forensic science through shows like *CSI: Crime Scene Investigation* now demand unreasonable levels of physical evidence in trials. Other jurors may actually think there is not "sufficient evidence" in a particular case (e.g., "Why is there no fingerprint evidence from the victim's body in this homicide?"). There is a responsibility associated with forensic science's commitment to serve social needs and values. Scientists who are aware of the influence to meet the needs and expectations of employers; feeling forced, threatened, or the need to pacify superiors can lead to poor ethical decisions. Finally, a major source of pressure is the preference for self-regulation in forensic science. Self-regulation requires greater internal control from every individual. Examples of individual misconduct include lying about degrees never earned or embellishing training and education received. Though forensic science is a high-pressure field that has many unusual stressors, it does not excuse unethical behavior.

The professional duties of forensic scientists are coupled with pressure. Unprofessional conduct includes any actions that may tarnish the reputation of an agency or enable the public to lose trust. An example is a case where management publicly denying that one of their scientists was drylabbing, even though he or she was in fact drylabbing, demonstrates unprofessional conduct leading to unethical conduct. Drylabbing is creating scientific data without performing any tests used in part to describe forensic laboratory actions of creating a report without performing tests on crime scene evidence. (www.statemaster.com/encyclopedia/drylabbing.) Some of the professional duties presenting ethical issues specifically for forensic scientists are as follows:

1. The duty to *remain competent* in a wide range of scientific fields, while often limited resources for library and professional meetings are available. If appropriate resources are not provided and the forensic scientist cannot meet his or her responsibility as a scientist, is it ethical to continue to present oneself as such?
2. The duty to be as *objective* as reasonably possible in the selection of samples, examinations, and the interpretation of results. Is it ethical to ignore relevant samples known to exist simply because they were not submitted? Can one refrain from certain significant tests on request and still be considered ethical?
3. The duty to act *thoroughly and to produce results* and conclusions within the capabilities and limitations of science and within the expertise of the individual scientist. Forensic science often involves examinations that are one of a kind. In these cases, is it ethical to not fully reveal the procedures used, the supporting data, or the result of blind trials? Is it ethical to use a procedure in the absence of such

data? How far is it necessary to go in explaining things that are critical scientifically but that may have little or no legal relevance? Should the reasons for inconclusive results not be explained?

4. The duty to be *openly communicative*. When open communication between scientists is restricted by the demands of others, the scientist is faced with an ethical dilemma. Is it ethical for the scientist not to publish the results of his or her research for the benefit of all? Should one refuse to talk to other scientists because they may have a different interpretation? Should scientists use a technique that has not received peer review?

Another area of scientific difficulty is having precision without accuracy. *Accuracy* is the degree of exactness possessed by an approximation or measurement, while *precision* is the degree of exactness with which a quantity is expressed. Although it is possible to have precision without accuracy and to have accuracy without being precise, the latter is actually the better situation. Accuracy is extremely important to forensic science; however, it has been argued that some forensic methods are more accurate than others. DNA is said to be the most accurate forensic evidence, while fingerprints are considered less accurate due to conclusions based on an examiner. A *precisionist* is a person who quotes exact numbers instead of giving approximations (99'10.78" as opposed to 100'). Although this person seems as though she is a wonderful scientist, juries may be wrongly seduced by this person. In addition, such precision is an excessive and ineffective action. The aforementioned dimensions are useful for crime scene sketches requiring accurate measurements of bullet holes or angles. However, such an example is unnecessary for parking lots because the nearest inch is usually sufficient (although it depends on what is measured). As with any ethical situation, best practices and personal judgment are reliable guiding factors (Garrison 2004).

The problem of practicing science in an adversary system is yet another reason why ethical dilemmas occur in forensic science. Some issues include the amount of detail tests or reports require and the amount of disclosure that the forensic scientist necessitates. An additional issue is how to decide what information needs to be presented. How does the information get presented? Should the expert offer "extra" information in which neither lawyer showed interest? What if additional information is pertinent to explain results? Unfortunately, these problems are nearly impossible to solve due to the conflicting goals of science and law. Knowledge of the differences may help each side overcome some common obstacles.

Unethical Behavior
The Fork in the Road

Know your ethical limits.

J. Hardwig

Introduction

Ethical dilemmas occur for many reasons, especially in forensic science. Within the overall culture, there is a lack of research and development that is directly related to the lack of funding available. Limited funding and resources promote a sense of scientists playing "catch up" as opposed to staying ahead of new technology, methods, or procedures. Competency problems may occur when individuals are overworked and overwhelmed. Many scientists are responsible for their own training and continuing education because the resources are not provided or available through agencies. Individuals bear the financial burden and time commitment to attend meetings and training and to read literature in their spare time, and they forego research. Are these good reasons for unethical behavior? No. Are they contributing factors? Yes. Misconduct may also occur due to the inability of agencies to separate from other professional cultures, such as law enforcement agencies. Although the structure may contribute to the pressure scientists face, it is an organizational issue and for all intents and purposes is out of the scientists' control. The best way to overcome such pressure is to understand the goals of the opposing culture and at times to agree to disagree. The most common form of individual misconduct is the misrepresentation of background or credentials—for instance, a person claiming a degree not earned or a professional affiliation not held. Other common forms of unethical behavior in forensic science include overstating the significance of findings, providing testimony beyond the examiner's expertise, and improperly preparing laboratory reports. This chapter explores ethical dilemmas and how people make wrong choices.

What if Leanne, as a new employee, is given an order that she knows is not 100% correct? Should she go against a direct order from her superior? Should she follow what the person told her to do? Should she do what she thinks is right regardless of what she was told? Should she report what she was told to do? If she does decide to report it, to whom should she report it? Maybe she should just mention it to another colleague as a "feeler"? How far should she go? What if no one else she talks to sees the issue? What if everyone turns on her for questioning a superior?

These are just some of the questions a person may have when making a decision. Factors to consider include the situation, the people involved, the potential consequences of actions (or inactions), and whether the decision is right for the person as an individual, a professional, and an ethical person. Ethical decision making involves at least four primary components: identifying the moral issues of the decision, understanding of standards that are applicable to the situation, being aware of the magnitude and complexity of such decisions, and being willing to make difficult decisions and stand by them. The complicated part about ethical decision making is choosing the best option when many solutions are possible. Although two people may have different solutions to a problem, it does not necessarily make one person wrong if the same ends are achieved. When confronted with an ethical dilemma, it is easy to "just deal with it" in the moment; however, this could cause a person to set aside principles to immediately solve the issue. In critical situations it is likely that a person would take the approach of doing what needs to be done now and worrying later. This method is suitable as long as the person is able to accept the same action if it were taken by someone else. Some important steps to avoid when making ethical decisions include relying on emotion and the popular choice and supporting immoral principles. In regards to science, what ethical dilemmas are faced? Are there moral limits to what scientific knowledge people should seek? When should people stop asking questions? What if knowledge is misused? Is knowledge about certain things harmful because people possess it or because people apply it in unintended ways?

There are many actions a person may take to solve ethical dilemmas. The first, in true scientific fashion, is to frame a set of questions and to gather relevant information. All options should be explored with intersubjectivity to view issues from alternate perspectives. The next step is the most difficult: Options need to be evaluated by assessing choices in light of obligation. Finally, a person should make a decision after considering factors such as if he or she could justify the action publicly, could count on anyone else to assist or make the decision for him or her, and if he or she could live comfortably with the decision. Recommendations for coping with ethical conflicts include remaining selfish about one's personal and professional reputation, not making ethics more difficult than they actually are, trusting "gut feelings" of uneasiness, and asking oneself what your mother would advise you to do. Once a decision is made, the person should take action. Typically in most situations there are a lack of standards so more dilemmas may arise. The process is based on making necessary accommodations and balancing pros and cons. Throughout the process, it is imperative to focus on the primary goals by exploring the issues, overcoming obstacles, making a case, and, finally, making a decision.

Ethical issues can make people feel "stuck" and leave them at a loss for making decisions. Sometimes few options are available or appealing. Many times people feel that a limited number of choices would help: A person could choose the lesser of the evils. Unfortunately, life is more complicated, and there are usually many avenues to explore. The best solution is to get creative and come up with alternate possibilities. There are professionals called "creative experts" who teach innovative methods in industry and management. This approach is useful to ethics because even if the expert's ideas are not the best fit for an agency, the thinking process is initiated. Creativity is especially significant when dealing with ethics because, as Weston (2001) states, "Narrow and limited questions leave us with narrow and limited answers." What is the best way to achieve creativity? The first idea is to *loosen up* because issues are more than just black and white. A good way to achieve this is to try a new approach, perhaps something that seems impossible. The next idea is to *talk to others* to see what they are doing. This is a good way to broaden your own horizon. It does not mean that you have to follow what is advised; it will simply serve as a fresh perspective. The next idea is to *brainstorm* without criticism. Even if the process does not produce expected results, it will provide several new options to consider. Creative thinking is ignited by "crazy ideas" or solutions that people would normally rule out. "What if" questions are a useful way to provoke the thought process—for example, what if the laboratory is falsely accused of wrongdoing, or what if a scientist did something wrong and confided in a colleague? Although an activity that could make a person fairly paranoid, it is useful in preparing for situations and in obtaining a better perspective of colleagues' thoughts and opinions on issues. The final idea on how to achieve creativity is to *shift the problem*. This idea encourages people to stop trying to solve the problem as they see it and instead to look at the cause of the problem. Instead of trying to fix the problem itself, could a person fix the cause of that problem? Could issues be prevented, if not solved? We must always remind ourselves that while there are other cases, people may not always have another chance to repair their integrity.

Unethical Behavior

People are required to make numerous choices each day, many of which have ethical components. As individuals we judge our own actions, as well as the actions of others, according to some standard. Although there is not a rule book for decisions, we each use information from our upbringing, family values, cultures, religious views, common sense, and best judgment to decide what is right or wrong. As a general rule, anything that dehumanizes a person is unethical because human beings are conscious of their actions and employ free will in making choices. Many times questions are asked that provide a clear picture of how complex the topic of ethics may become, such as, "Everyone knows that _____ (any behavior) is unethical, so why even talk about it?" or "Isn't it unethical to judge the ethics of others?" or "My parents did a good job, so why should I learn things that I already know?" It is insufficient to assume that people develop personal ethics that always lead them to engage in ethical behavior; however, empathy for people in ethical dilemmas may encourage support and clarity of issues. Although ethical judgments are based on individual opinion and there is not necessarily a right or wrong answer, some general guidelines may help:

- Do not use misinformation to support claims.
- Do not represent yourself as an expert if you are not.
- Do not use misleading or unfounded reasoning.
- Do not divert attention away from an issue.
- Do not misuse people's emotions by presenting topics that have little to do with the main idea.
- Do not deceive people of your intentions, viewpoints, or purpose.
- Do not hide potential consequences, positive or negative.
- Do not oversimplify issues to convolute a point.
- Do not advocate for things that you do not support.

The guidelines, while general, are a good place to start making decisions. Many times it is difficult for people to objectively view a situation and the potential consequences if they are too close to the situation. It is helpful when a person is as objective as possible or can receive input from an impartial person. Sensitivity to ethical decisions requires people to examine their behaviors, principles, and goals. Unethical situations occur, so it is important to examine the factors that lead to unethical behavior, the types of situations that become unethical, and the common pressures that cause people to make bad choices. It is stressed that *everyone is human and all humans make mistakes*, but it does not hurt to have an awareness of potential issues, how to avoid them, and how to manage problems that do occur, especially before the problems escalate. Specifically, professional organizations and agencies need to take an ethical stance, have a willingness to confront ethical problems, and maintain values indicative of organizational standards. Ethical role models in leadership positions encourage staff members to take responsibility for their actions, treat people fairly and with compassion, participate in open communication, and show respect to one another. This is not to say that leaders are exempt from ethical misconduct;

however, they have the ability to influence the culture of a workplace. No matter how much a person knows, if the circumstances are "right," anyone could make a bad decision. It is how the person handles the decision once it is made that determines if ethical lines are crossed, how far the situation is taken, who is impacted, and if redemption is possible.

Forensic scientists encounter many occupational hazards regarding ethical behavior. The positions within forensic science are complex and come with high stress and public trust. There is a great need for coping mechanisms due to being surrounded by crime and death. There is potential for dishonesty due to the regular dealings with money, drugs, and weapons. Forensic scientists must constantly gain new knowledge to keep up with current problems. Though it is the scientists' job to report findings, they may not have a say in how decision makers interpret and twist the facts that they provide. Forensic scientists must function within legal constraints while accepting ultimate responsibility for their conduct. Some professional duties of forensic scientists may challenge ethical performance—for example, obstacles with evidence presented by attorneys. Unfortunately, some selective bias is unavoidable and almost expected by the legal system. Additional duties that present ethical issues are the duty to remain competent in a wide range of scientific fields with (often) limited resources; the duty to remain as objective as reasonably possible in the selection of samples, examinations, and the interpretation of results; the duty to work thoroughly and produce results and conclusions within the capabilities and limitations of science and themselves; and the duty to communicate openly. Aside from all the factors mentioned, there is the responsibility and pressure to become familiar with the professional cultures that coexist with forensic science, which have been discussed. Considering the many factors that impact ethical decisions, it is not surprising that issues do occur.

The frequency of misconduct in science is very low compared with business, law, or medicine; however, misconduct still remains part of the scientific culture. Though the examples of unethical behavior within science may not be numerous, what they lack in quantity they make up for in severity. Forensic science is work that could seriously impact people's lives if not conducted with the utmost integrity. During the 17 years that he was on the American Academy of Forensic Sciences Ethics Committee, Doug Lucas states that over 50 complaints were investigated and about half were eventually dismissed. Some examples of misconduct in science are lying, cheating, stealing, falsification, fabrication, plagiarism, defamation, misrepresentation, distortion, and deliberate deception. Falsification differs from fabrication in that the former involves *tampering* with evidence or results while the latter involves actually *making up* the information. Is it ever ethical to lie? What if a lie spares someone's feelings? What if the lie keeps a person out of harm's way? More often than not, the misconduct starts on a small scale, such as a "little white lie," and intensifies. Issues of misconduct may arise because science is a cooperative activity within a large social and political context. It is also common that scientists may not agree with the standards set forth by the profession. Discipline-specific standards relating to error are important. There is a fine line between ethical and unethical practices, so it is imperative that scientists exercise scientific, practical, and moral judgment and disclose any actual or potential conflicts.

In addition to some of the more common forms of misconduct, other types should be considered. The first, *conflict of conscience,* arises when a scientist with deeply held personal views is asked to review projects whose nature is offensive to his or her viewpoints. Basically, issues occur when the convictions of an individual are permitted to override scientific merit in reaching a decision. In health sciences, patient care constantly faces changing patterns of medical ethics regarding premature births, life support, pain control, and assisted suicide. Unlike conflicts of interest, conflicts of conscience do not involve personal gain or affect assigned duties. This conflict is also represented by the ambiguous boundary between inappropriate incentives and acceptable perks. For example, handouts or giveaways at meetings are routine, accepted, and typically expected, but expensive meals and gifts provided by vendors cross the line. As of now there is no agreement on how to handle these conflicts, mostly because society is ever changing. Luckily, this type of conflict is not as prevalent in forensic science as it is in other fields, such as law enforcement.

Conflicts of effort, or *conflicts of commitment,* may arise when demands made by people other than the primary employer interfere with the performance of the employees' assigned duties. Examples of this type of pressure include presenting lectures, serving on boards and panels, or teaching, all of which are usually encouraged activities. Scientists usually know how to prioritize responsibilities, but unscheduled tasks can put an added demand on people, especially if the tasks are agency mandated. Typically, the immediate supervisor is responsible for deployment of staff to other projects. Extra duties can become a serious issue when scientists are not available for their assigned tasks. Conflicts of effort frequently occur when scientists have for-profit businesses or the extreme ambition to gain acceptance within the field (i.e., are on every committee possible and refuse to miss meetings). Although people may say that some agencies send mixed messages by allowing one day per week for such "extra" tasks, it is an excellent way to alleviate conflicts. Time is allotted for extra tasks separate from one's everyday tasks, which makes the situation much more "workable." The scientific community presents many opportunities for excellence, which unfortunately contributes to the frequency of conflicts of effort as people try to build their credentials and accolades. Awareness and standards of conduct for such situations will lessen conflicts of effort.

Money tends to increase occurrences of ethical misconduct. A person or a group that receives payment multiple times for a job is "double-dipping." This conflict is one of the most common because people do not necessarily know that their salary is inclusive for all of the work they do, including research and sometimes teaching or presentations. In addition, if the scientists are paid from multiple sources, their total efforts from all projects cannot add up to more than 100%. This seems like common sense, but it is fairly routine that people, especially researchers, are funded from a variety of sources and may or may not know the division. Compensation in forensic science mostly involves speaker and consultant fees. Speakers may require fees or honorariums and travel or lodging accommodations. Guidelines may vary between agencies, but scientists should understand the standard procedures of the agency before committing to the way they may think is best. Consultant compensation is subject to approval by employers. Scientists must avoid not only conflicts of interest but also the mere appearance of conflicts of interest when employers are negotiating consulting contracts with private organizations on their behalf. It is every scientist's personal responsibility to disclose consulting services to employers and to assure that conflicts of interest are not an issue.

The final type of unethical behavior is favoritism. Favoritism shown to experts, consultants, or editors occurs often. Reasons may include easygoing personality, likeability by juries, minimal fees for service, being willing to adjust results to support a theory, being highly respected in the field, or simply being excellent at one's job. Favoritism shown to relatives or close friends, or *nepotism*, is a concern in any field. Business, politics, and entertainment create the highest frequency of nepotism complaints. Most professions have rules against nepotism to ensure fairness for potential employees. However, many people are actually in support of nepotism. The American Association of University Professors has called for the discontinuation of policies that prohibit professional opportunities for members of an immediate family. In the article "Nepotism Pays," Ferrazzi states his belief that a person can create his or her own nepotism. It is about having three things: (1) superior access to people in power; (2) the deepest care and concern from people who could potentially speed another person to success; and then (3) sufficient skill. Ferrazzi is making steps to change the negative connotation of nepotism; however, it is still considered a conflict of interest in science and research. Nepotism may occur in forensic science in a variety of ways. One example is if a higher-ranking family member always gives higher priority or more interesting cases to a coworker that is a relative. Another example is demonstrated by relatives or friends getting assigned to the "easier" cases by higher-ranking family members or friends. Although not as prevalent as other forms of misconduct, nepotism can and does occur. After having explored ways ethical misconduct occurs, let us now look at why issues may occur.

Motivation

The various forensic science occupations have unique features that may contribute to unethical behaviors. Factors such as high public trust, acting as good role models, high stress, versatility of job positions, the need for coping mechanisms, and the potential for corruption are all possible sources of unethical behavior among those in the laboratory, at the crime scene, or in law enforcement. Television shows like *CSI: Crime Scene Investigation* put increased pressure on crime scene personnel and police officers to provide "forensic" evidence. The Hollywood version of forensic science also shapes the public's perception of the relationships among science, law enforcement, and the judicial system. High-profile cases such as that of O. J. Simpson or JonBenet Ramsey thrust forensic scientists into the limelight. These situations may provide the opportunity for media attention and payment for expert opinions while creating an opening for society to scrutinize forensic science practices. Influences for unethical behavior are cultural, individual, and organizational. Cultural influences include beliefs in the possibility of change, beliefs about how laws affect behavior, and tolerance for other cultures and viewpoints. Individual influences include fear, vulnerability, and claims that certain situations are not as important as others. Finally, organizational influences encourage fear of open discussion and may create overconfident and complacent employees. Many motivating factors contribute to unethical behavior in forensic science.

The path to unethical conduct depends on factors such as how people view themselves, their careers, and the world. These attitudes or beliefs precede behavior, action, and conduct. People that act unethically commonly underestimate the likelihood that the truth will eventually come out. In addition, these people overestimate their ability to manage the situation or to succumb to pressure. Often, cases that are in the headlines begin when someone decides to cut a corner for what seems like a good reason at the time. Unfortunately, the next time the corner becomes sharper and the incidents more severe and frequent until the pattern is discovered. Some motives to unethical behavior may include a sense of entitlement, demanding management, momentum, shrinking budgets, inappropriate pressures on forensic scientists, or simply that it works! Privacy, anonymity, and autonomy may influence a person to feel "safe." If a person feels as though his or her behavior is not monitored, he or she may attempt to get away with actions that are against the rules. Chances for unethical behavior will also increase during times of agency restructuring or growth. The most probable time for unethical behavior is when there is a disparity in ethical codes; this often happens in crime laboratories that are a subset of police departments. It is expected that a greater number of incidences occur during times of undue command or "cultural" influence, when laboratories have excessive caseloads or backlog, and when scientists are inadequately trained.

A person's motivation to act unethically may include a variety of factors. It is important to first assess the person's character by talking with him or her and the person's colleagues. The next step is to examine the person's previous work to determine if there is a pattern of dishonesty. How people respond to allegations—for example, do they lie low or go out of their way to show their positive attributes—provides a good indication of whether misconduct has occurred. In addition to the factors mentioned earlier that fuel unethical behavior, it is also important to consider reasons that are based on human factors. The following motives are associated with scientists in the role of expert witnesses:

- Competition: Some people in the legal system may see their actions, and the consequences to those actions, as a game.
- Job security: Specifically for the self-employed, such as independent experts or consultants.
- Economic reward: When an expert receives payment to testify about something with the sole purpose of confusing the issues to damage the opposing side's case.
- Principle: When one expert testifies against another for unprofessional motivations such as revenge, spite, or economic reward.
- Recognition: Forensic scientists may seek recognition and work only high-profile cases.
- Ego: Some experts may feel that they do not need to prepare as thoroughly for testimony on some subjects because of who they are, the background they have, or the type of cases they work.

Please note that there are many types of expert witnesses: Some experts are paid to consult and provide an expert opinion, whereas others testify as part of their job duties. The aforementioned motives more frequently represent consultant experts but may also apply to public forensic scientists.

The trainer–trainee relationship is an excellent example of informal instruction that creates gray areas and influences misconduct in a professional setting. Such relationships do not always have set guidelines, which may introduce opportunities for misconduct. Trainers or mentors may exploit new employees because of the unbalanced relationship, professional status, experience, and knowledge. In addition to the inequality, factors such as a lack of time spent with the mentor, the feeling that one is seen as a burden by the mentor, and the possibility for discrimination may impair the trainee's ability to receive adequate training. Rules and standards assure that the mentor–trainee relationship is closely monitored to avoid problems and to foster the development of a professional. Instruction in regards to policies, procedures, actions, consequences, and the overall professional culture occurs informally but should foster professionalism and prevent misconduct. To prevent trainees from getting led astray, managers need to choose mentors who will influence professionalism and decrease the gray area for trainees. These areas occur when there is more than one right answer or method, during which people must choose what is *most* right. People often disagree as to what appropriate behaviors are in given situations. Adherence to a code of ethics does not necessarily ensure competence, but it does help to provide a clear understanding of ethical violations. This understanding also provides a basis for people to determine the impact of potential unethical conduct. Defining the ethical obligations for a profession allows mentors to determine the values associated within the professional culture.

The forensic profession is composed of many disciplines and subfields all having their own policies, procedures, and goals. In the laboratory, the scientific method is held as the guide for all scientific experiments. Although the term *scientific method* implies that there is one specific process, the method actually consists of prescribed steps. The steps in forensic science include the use of all potential examinations, the use of many sources of information, the use of error rates and uncertainty, and objective, thorough examinations used to gain information from evidence. Although having only one source of data is a good way to eliminate gray areas, it is not a realistic way to remain unbiased. If evidence points in one direction, it is best to observe sources of information that may contradict and lead in a different direction. The variation may either reinforce or negate the scientists' results. One of the main dynamics in science is uncertainty. Any high-quality attorney will lead the triers-of-fact to believe that uncertainty is negative; however, it is common and expected in science. Uncertainty is an event with unknown probability. In science, uncertainty is a given characteristic of all information that scientists must acknowledge and communicate.

In science, gray areas may occur with evidence that is significant in one region or laboratory but of no interest to another. For example, soil evidence found in Connecticut and traced back to New Mexico is significant because the locations have different soil types. Scientists must then examine how and why the soil from one location ended up in the other location. The same soil evidence that came from New Mexico would not have the significance in a case from New Mexico because the soil is common to the area. In the second case, the soil evidence represents a gray area that does not lead scientists to a specific conclusion: The evidence is neither positive nor negative; it simply does not have a right answer in regards to the case. Gray areas are unavoidable; however, standards are in place to ease the burden of decisions regarding actions or methods that are "more right."

Some people truly do not understand why their actions are considered unethical. Personality traits may influence the misinterpretation between right and wrong actions. *Dogmatist* represents the first type of personality. People with this personality are committed to one answer and will not change their minds. In general, people are committed to an idea and cannot recognize alternatives, which does not allow for adaptable decision making. People should listen to other people's perspectives, seek arguments for the opposing side, examine reasons for having alternate positions, and adjust language to be neutral to avoid dogmatism. The next personality type to explore is those who participate in *offhand self-justification*. These people automatically make excuses or become defensive when questioned. Steps toward prevention of this natural response include personal reminders of how self-defeating the reaction is, awareness of the anger or irritation one might feel, and avoidance of instinctive counterattacks. The final personality type to discuss is *relativism* or when a person believes that not one single standard is "right." People with this type of personality tend to think "it's all relative" and that what is right for one person may not be right for another. Although people with this personality type do not usually view their actions as unethical, they need to take accountability for actions based on whatever personal and professional standards they follow. Relativism, more than any other personality type, introduces the likelihood of personal ethics that clash with professional ethics. Unethical decisions occur for a variety of reasons, most of which people are able to rationalize.

Justification

People typically draw on their existing frames of reference to excuse, justify, or rationalize unethical behavior. Frames of reference may include role models, mentors, cultural influences, religious influences, experience, knowledge, or training. People may also draw on the elements of society to rationalize or excuse negative behavior. Societal influences include the media, politicians, lawmakers, and the ambiguity of laws. Justification of unethical behaviors occurs passively or actively. Passive justification occurs when people evade ethical responsibility. Some examples include the following thoughts: "I did what I was told to do"; "It was part of my job to do it"; "Everyone else is"; "My actions won't make a difference in the grand scheme of things"; "It is not my problem"; and "Nobody knew about it, so it doesn't matter." Many times omission (doing nothing to prevent or stop unethical behavior) is just as bad as the commission of unethical actions. If misconduct occurs unintentionally, a person should publicly acknowledge his or her mistakes so others are aware that the action or consequences were unintentional. Active justification occurs many times through self-deception, which includes false beliefs, willful ignorance, and avoidance. Self-deception is a considerable problem because a person creates so many lies that he or she actually starts to believe the false details. In addition, self-deception may contribute to a person's increased self-confidence; in a normal situation this is a positive outcome, but here it is negative because the confidence is based on dishonesty.

Another way people maintain a positive self-image is through the use of techniques of neutralization (more detail can be found in Braswell, McCarthy, and McCarthy, 2005). The first technique is *denial of injury* where a person justifies actions based on whether anyone has been hurt because of his or her actions. The second technique is *denial of the victim* where a person denies an action is wrong based on the circumstance; victims are characterized socially into groups such as good or bad, dangerous or friendly. The next technique is *condemning the condemners* where a person shifts the attention from his or her acts of misconduct to the motives and behaviors of those who allege misconduct has occurred. The final technique of neutralization that a person engaging in unethical behavior may take is an *appeal to higher loyalties*. This technique is the most powerful and causes severe unethical behavior by sacrificing the demands of society for the demands of a smaller social group. When working with other professional cultures, as forensic scientists commonly do, justifying bad behaviors by claiming they are widely accepted within one's culture is wrong. Justifying acts by stating that the opposing culture's actions are much worse and asserting superiority over the other culture is even worse. Throughout the process of justification people should analyze their own conscience, examine precedents, and openly debate the issue. People sometimes view ethical matters as irrelevant unless they directly impact others. It is easy for people to remove themselves from responsibility or to disregard ethical considerations when they feel they need something, deserve something, or think that no one will know the action took place because the consequences will not affect anyone.

Consequences

Ethical misconduct has both personal and professional consequences. Such actions threaten teamwork, morale, and productivity within an agency and the self-respect of a scientist. Cases of unethical behavior create negative publicity and impact the entire profession. Previous cases, research, and established reputations become tarnished. The image of science becomes flawed when misconduct, or even "alleged" misconduct, is uncovered. Expert testimony is scrutinized more closely, and its value is potentially jeopardized by misconduct within the field. Although recovery from misconduct is possible, it is unbelievably difficult, takes a long time, and requires enormous effort to regain the public's trust. Many situations have no "right" answer regarding what is ethically appropriate and this can hinder a person's ability to resolve a situation that had no clear answers from the start.

Codes of conduct for the profession and the organization help to prevent people from taking unethical actions. Primary steps for prevention of misconduct taken by the forensic science community include proficiency testing, professional codes of ethics, American Society of Crime Laboratory Directors-Laboratory Accreditation Board (ASCLD-LAB) accreditation guidelines, and the American Society of Crime Laboratory Directors (ASCLD) management guidelines. Accreditation guidelines focus on the laboratory system, not on individuals, which makes training and continuing education even more important for laboratory employees. The efforts listed will not help people who are intent on fraud; however, they will provide opportunities for people to better observe the work and conduct of colleagues. Studies have shown that people are not severely punished if they are suspected of making unintentional, honest mistakes. Even though humans tend to feel responsibility only for the actions we *intend* to occur, we are ethically responsible for all of our actions. The best way to avoid the consequences of unethical actions is to avoid misconduct altogether. While this is easier said than done in some cases, one should remember that it is much easier in the long run to behave ethically than it is to cheat. When the truth is upheld, one does not have to remember all of the stories and excuses used regarding actions and motives. In the case of Martha Stewart, she was not convicted for insider trading; she was convicted for lying about her actions. Misconduct can have a profound effect on the work that is conducted so it is important to regulate behaviors before they are taken as misconduct.

The scientific culture is vulnerable to misconduct that could seriously impact the profession; because of this, there are standards that assist in decreasing the frequency of problems. Self-correcting mechanisms within the scientific culture include the use of a scientific method, peer review, publication, and the open communication between science and society. Unfortunately, such procedures do not always find fraud or error, though they may catch mistakes. Science is a human institution and mistakes are human nature, so it is important that the processes in place can differentiate between misconduct and unintentional errors. There is some concern over accepted practices and deviation from those practices because the methods used to evaluate a person's intentions are open to broad interpretation. In attempting to decrease scientific misconduct, more focus should be on the context in which scientists work as opposed to potential errors in their work. Scientists are a direct reflection of their agency. Ethically good agencies foster duty, integrity, self-control, and democracy as guiding principles. The integrity of an agency or laboratory is based on its employees' knowledge of ethical principles and their desire to act in good faith. Knowledge is based on experience, education, training, awareness of policies, and involvement with professional organizations. The desire to act in good faith is based on a person's history with honesty; managerial experience in doing the "right thing"; and the ethical courage of agency leaders in making hard decisions, facilitating conflict resolution, and encouraging open communication. Scientists who are aware of the guidelines and principles that regulate the field and their specific discipline decrease the chance of misconduct occurring. How does someone decide who is responsible for unethical conduct? The most important regulation that scientists receive for their work is reviews by scientists working in the same discipline. Forensic scientists have an obligation and responsibility to the suspects, victims, friends, and family members involved in cases to objectively analyze evidence and to present honest opinions and conclusions.

Whistle-Blowing

Whistle-blowing is defined as "conveying information about a serious moral problem in one's organization outside approved organizational channels to someone in a position to take action, either inside or outside the organization" (Martin 2007, p. 65). Some additional information to add to the definition is that whistle-blowing "might consist of communicating information against organizational pressures, such as wishes of supervisors and colleagues" (Martin 2007, p. 65). Members of organizations may participate in unethical actions that Frederick Bird (1996) describes as moral silence, moral deafness, and moral blindness. *Moral silence* is the avoidance of whistle-blowing by persons not voicing objections, not advocating ideals, and not holding others sufficiently accountable for their actions. *Moral deafness* is when people are not willing to listen; people lack focus on the most important points of a situation, avoid hearing bad news, and may not understand a situation because of inappropriate assumptions. *Moral blindness* involves losing sight of issues or problems by overlooking consequences. It may also involve ignoring obligations, promises, principles, and expectations because of bias or stereotypes. The result of moral deafness, silence, and blindness includes unaddressed issues, little to no accountability or responsibility for actions, moral stress, and a confused role of ethics. Most organizations do maintain an "open door" policy for free communication in theory, but in practice there are pressures against challenging colleagues. Science has little need for whistle-blowing because science is self-correcting; retesting experiments reveals potential problems. Science is a profession that depends on the commitment to truth because the work conducted primarily builds on work of others. If necessary, whistle-blowing does fall within the scientist's obligation to help others and the profession. Whistle-blowing also serves individuals by helping them maintain their responsibility as ethical professionals. Whistle-blowing has limits and exceptions—including obligations to employers and colleagues—so it is important to make sure that whistle-blowing is the appropriate action for a given situation.

A whistle-blower is a person who reports unethical or illegal conduct or wrongdoing outside of normal internal communication to publicly expose problems faced by an organization regarding ethics, legality, or safety. This person is typically courageous and holds high personal and professional standards. Studies have shown that women are actually less likely than men to act as whistle-blowers. *Time Magazine* did a piece on three female whistle-blowers for the annual "Persons of the Year" article in 2002, one of whom brought attention to misconduct that was occurring in the Federal Bureau of Investigation (FBI). Examples and further information are provided in the next chapter. They may be viewed as a hero or as a traitor, but there is a strong negative connotation involved with whistle-blowers, so before taking action a person should consider the following points:

- Am I fairly and accurately depicting the seriousness of the problem?
- Have I secured the information properly, analyzed it appropriately, and presented it fairly?
- Do my motives spring from serving a public need more than from serving a personal desire?
- Have I fully tried to have the problem corrected within the organization?
- Should I blow the whistle while still a member of the organization or after having left it?
- Should I reveal my identity or keep it secret?
- Have I made claims with proper intensity and with appropriate frequency?
- How ethical have I been in selecting my audience?
- How ethical is it for me, a participant in the functioning of the group, to assume the role of the judge?
- How ethical is it to set into motion an act that will likely be very costly to many people (emotionally and financially)?
- How neutral have I been in choosing my audience?
- Who am I to judge?
- Am I living up to the standard of the organization and colleagues (loyalty)?
- Am I ethical according to the profession?
- How will my actions affect my family and affiliates?
- Am I true to myself, my integrity, and my well-being?
- How will this affect basic human values (e.g., freedom, courage, loyalty, judgment)?

Once a person decides to blow the whistle, there are guidelines to follow to report the suspected misconduct. First, the person should have morally good motives. In other words, the person should make a report to describe illegal, unethical, or immoral actions, not to advance his or her own career or harm a rival. It has been reported that about half of whistle-blowers act from questionable motives and evidence that can damage the reputation of the whistle-blower, the targeted individuals, or the organization. Those who suspect fraud do not always have solid proof and if they make claims, counter claims of disloyalty are often brought against them. Egos and defective collaborations complicate the process and validity of whistle-blowing. False claims or claims from people with corrupt motives may desensitize managers to reports of unethical behavior.

The next guideline in reporting misconduct is the person should have some well-documented evidence before making accusations. The evidence should include more than hearsay or personal observations. Also, the person should make accusations to the relevant authorities and go outside the organization only as a last resort. Potential repercussions for the whistle-blower are possibly avoided by going to the proper authority as well as preventing in-house gossip. Finally, the person should carefully deliberate his or her actions and avoid a rush to judgment. Sometimes things are not what they seem; however, even actions perceived as unethical may be considered so regardless of the truth.

There are three stages of social confrontation of unethical behavior: preconfrontation, initial confrontation, and postconfrontation. Preconfrontation is the step in which witnesses assure that they are in fact witnessing the behavior they believe is occurring, assess the severity of the action, monitor the behavior of those involved in the behavior, and talk with others to determine if anyone else has observed the behavior and to gauge if colleagues feel the issue is important to prevent. The person also decides if the unethical action requires urgent attention, analyzes the relationship between himself or herself and the accused, decides whether confrontation is his or her responsibility, anticipates the accused person's reaction, determines what personal resources he or she needs to invest, decides on the appropriate time and place for confrontation, and decides the costs versus rewards of confrontation. During the initial confrontation, the witness informs the accused that he or she violated a rule or standard. The phrasing used by the witness sets the tone, so he or she must be cautious of accusation and blame. Finally, postconfrontation may occur after the initial confrontation if the need arises. Guidelines serve to aid people in reporting misconduct.

In 2005, a study of 3,000 Americans with a wide range of jobs in a variety of agencies was conducted by the National Business Ethics Survey. The results showed that one-third of those surveyed had encountered a situation that invited ethical misconduct. A total of 75% of those individuals reported witnessing one or more incidents of misconduct. The most common types of misconduct noted were intimidating behavior and lying. Only half of those people actually reported misconduct. People who reported misconduct cited the belief that correction would occur, the support of management and coworkers, and the belief that it was the right thing to do as reasons for their report. People who did not report the misconduct they witnessed believed that nothing would be done, had a fear of retaliation, thought someone else would speak up, or did not know the proper procedures for reporting misconduct (Johannesen 2008). One of the reasons whistle-blowers are seen as courageous individuals is because many of them face negative consequences for their actions.

Oftentimes reporting misconduct has a negative effect on the reporter, even though he or she is obeying his or her ethical duty to speak up if unethical behavior is suspected. Possible repercussions, such as losing one's job, may make a person less likely to report misconduct. Professional cultures impose negativity toward whistle-blowers. In addition, there are unspoken pressures against challenging those in positions of authority by uncovering misconduct. Organizations should have procedures in place for scientists to request a case review or reexamination if something does not seem right. Aside from common pressures, a person may place a greater value on loyalty, which may account for why someone would withhold information regarding misconduct. Despite legal and institutional protections, it is likely that people who wish to report unethical conduct in science will have to choose between blowing the whistle and protecting their own personal interests. Such interests refer to their job, reputation, or friendships. Due to the potential negative consequences, it is helpful for agencies to have standards in place for reporting misconduct before they are needed.

Research shows that the complaints reported to forensic science associations are unrepresentative of the actual problems. The most frequent problem noted in forensic science is the misrepresentation of qualifications. Cases of litigation-related ethical issues are rare in reports yet seem common in practice. Another issue involves distortion of evidence by overstating conclusions, going beyond the scope of the evidence, or weighing evidence at a higher degree than necessary. These examples represent the most common unethical behaviors reported to professional associations of forensic science.

What if reporting misconduct has severe consequences for you?

Good Examples of Bad Behavior

7

O. J. Simpson Case

Throughout history there have been high-profile criminal cases. In the 1600s there were the Salem witch trials and in the 1890s was the Lizzie Borden case. More recently, each decade has been marked by particularly shocking high-profile cases: The 1960s had the Black Panthers movement; the 1970s provided the Charles Manson murders and Watergate scandal; the 1980s saw John Hinckley Jr.'s attempt at assassinating President Ronald Reagan; and the 1990s will be remembered for the Menendez brothers' killing of their parents, the beating of Rodney King and the Los Angeles riots that followed, and the O. J. Simpson trial. In recent years we have experienced the disappearances of Laci Peterson, Natalee Hollaway, and Caylee Anthony.

No other case dominated the media's attention over such an extended period of time as the O. J. Simpson trial, which became known as the "trial of the century." It has been suggested that the judge let pretrial publicity get out of hand. Whether this is true, the impact of the case itself, the overwhelming media attention, and the focus that the trial would create for forensic scientists and law enforcement were not anticipated.

This case is of particular importance regarding forensic ethics because the physical and scientific evidence were the primary focus. The first major issue was that the medical examiner's (ME) office personnel did not respond to the scene (at the request of the police) until approximately 10 hours after the victims were discovered. This is significant because it is the responsibility of the ME's office to arrive at the crime scene as soon as possible and to assure that evidence is properly collected and preserved. In addition, the delay in their arrival caused the holdup in determining the time of death, which resulted in a broader, less accurate range. During the pretrial hearing, the ME admitted mistakes in not having a representative investigator or pathologist on scene sooner. Under cross-examination at the hearing, 30–40 errors or mishandled evidence were discovered. The information supported the defense's claim that Simpson was being framed by officers. To save their case, prosecutors did not call the ME as a witness in the trial because he was such an embarrassment during preliminary hearings. Instead, the prosecution had the ME's boss testify even though he was not the one to conduct the autopsies; because most of his testimony was based on conjecture, his role was merely to support the prosecution's theory about what occurred during the crime. The State's primary case established reasonable certainty that Simpson had motive, means for the murders through a lack of alibi, and the presence of Simpson at the scene with the use of DNA and blood. The defense countered the prosecution's lack of alibi with expert witnesses that suggested the murders could have occurred much later than the prosecution stated. The defense also accused police of stealing blood samples to plant them at the scene. Based on this, the defense stated that the prosecution's DNA results were due to contamination; therefore, the blood and DNA evidence establishing the presence of Simpson at the scene needed to be dismissed. In addition to these key arguments, the trial included matches of DNA that were leaked to the press, over 1,000 exhibits presented, 126 witnesses testified, and a jury that was sequestered for 225 days.

The next major issue that was a focus of the Simpson trial was Detective Mark Fuhrman, who perjured himself on the stand. This occurred when the detective stated he had not used racial slurs in more than 10 years. Unfortunately for him, the defense obtained recordings of him using such language more recently than 10 years prior. The two primary issues in this trial were accompanied by many, much smaller yet more significant issues that were not given the proper time or attention. Many things were learned from this case regarding law enforcement and forensic science. The trial educated the general population as to the rules of the law such as what is truly meant by the phrases *innocent until proven guilty* and *beyond a reasonable doubt*. It taught society about the fields of forensic science and pathology and the use of DNA. Spousal abuse was exposed as an important topic that requires attention. Finally, the trial provided an exemplar as to what can be and is legitimately expected from the U.S. legal system. Although the trial brought professional issues into focus, it is not the appropriate standard to which society should judge the criminal justice system or the forensic science profession. The Simpson case was an anomaly, not the norm. The trial is in the history books much to the chagrin of the forensic community; however, it did provide a basis for the need for standards, validation, continuing education, and the study of ethics for forensic scientists and related professionals (Shiffman 2000).

Case Studies

False Credentials (Associated Press, 2007a)

This example involves a police ballistic expert who worked in the field for over 40 years: a very well-respected colleague named Dr. Joseph Kopera. It was revealed that he did not hold degrees from the Rochester Institute of

Technology or the University of Maryland as he had claimed in numerous court cases. Kopera estimated that he testified approximately 100–125 times per year. He became the supervisor of the state police firearms and tool marks unit in 2000 and managed their Integrated Ballistic Identification System (IBIS). As a result of the question concerning his credentials, the head of the state police worked with the Bureau of Alcohol, Tobacco, and Firearms (ATF) to review all of Kopera's violent crime cases. There was also an internal investigation to confirm the credentials of 40 forensic scientists and 16 crime scene technicians in the crime laboratory.

In reference to the allegations, many public defenders commented on the severity of the issue. Suzanne Drouet said, "Someone who has gone to the lengths to create a false background … will go to some lengths to fabricate information about the ballistics evidence itself." Michelle Nethercott, another public defender who is also the chief attorney in Maryland for the Innocence Project, stated that someone who would lie about credentials and then produce a fake document to support that fabrication may also have been "extremely helpful about filling in the blanks" for police to get a guaranteed conviction and that he showed "questionable accuracy" in transcripts from some former cases. On the other hand, Joe Cassilly, Harford County state's attorney, thought that the lack of degree was not enough to question evidence from past cases because much of an expert's knowledge is gained through on-the-job experience. In addition, the degrees in question were not needed for the job when Kopera was hired.

- What do you think?
- Does misinformation about one topic mean that the person will lie about anything?
- Do you think the omission was intentional?
- Should his past cases come into question? If so, should all cases receive review or just the violent crimes? Who decides? Upon what is your opinion based?
- Can you think of any circumstances that support the theory that these allegations were blown out of proportion? Or is it safer to assume that Kopera had malicious intent?

This example ends sadly; just weeks after the allegations were made and Kopera was confronted with the evidence, he was found dead from a self-inflicted gunshot wound at his home in Baltimore.

- Imagine that you were a friend and colleague of Dr. Kopera's. What impression would his death have on you?
- Would you likely believe that it was an admission of guilt?

- Would you think that he was genuinely a "good guy" and, after years of experience, just did not believe that the falsification was important at this point in his career?
- Would you think that justice was served because what he did was wrong, no matter the reason?

Misleading Degree (Moran, 2006)

This example involves a San Diego criminalist who falsely described his degree on his resume. Ray Cole testified as an expert in Driving Under the Influence (DUI) cases for over 30 years. During a routine audit on employees, the San Diego Sheriff's Department Crime Laboratory discovered the dishonesty. Although Cole claimed that he had a degree from the University of California–Berkeley in premedical studies, he actually received his degree in political science.

The following positions were taken by colleagues, attorneys, and superiors.

Pros

- The strength of his testimony was based on his experience, not what he studied in college.
- How is a false statement made on his resume going to have a significant effect on his testimony about whether a suspect was intoxicated?
- When he was hired in 1974, a degree was not a requirement for his position.
- The supervising criminalist listened to audio tapes of Cole's testimony in a particular case and confirmed that Cole did not testify to having a degree in premedical studies.

Cons

- Complaints have been filed against Cole from defense attorneys and prosecutors.
- Cole misrepresenting himself directly affects his credibility as a witness.
- When willing to lie about one thing, who is to say that the person will not lie about other things?
- Although the supervising criminalist listened to audiotapes of Cole's testimony in a particular case and confirmed that Cole did not testify to having a degree in premedical studies, that was only one case.
- Is this a real issue or not?

- Does the fact that a degree was not necessary for his position at the time he was hired make you feel better or worse about the situation? Why?
- Is it a convenient fact that it was stated that the attorneys had complaints about him prior to this discovery yet there is not more detail about this?
- Does misinformation about one topic mean that the person will lie about anything?
- Do you think the omission was intentional?
- Should his past cases come into question?

Abuse of Power (North, 2001)

This example concerns Michael Hoover, a Washington State Patrol chemist who allegedly stole heroin present in the laboratory. Coworkers were concerned about his unwavering insistence to work heroin cases, which encouraged patrol detectives to investigate with the help of hidden cameras. Once discovered, he admitted to ingesting heroin to lessen back pain he was experiencing and said that it began unintentionally. Hoover accidentally sniffed crystalline dust that was left behind after a test on evidence. When he realized that it provided relief for his back pain, he began sniffing small amounts of heroin that he purified in the laboratory. After 11 years as a forensic scientist, Hoover was placed on paid administrative leave, and more than 200 dismissals of drug cases were expected in one county alone.

He was charged with official misconduct and tampering with physical evidence, both of which carry maximum sentences of 12 months in jail. Felony charges were considered but not accepted because Hoover was not actually caught with drugs.

Although defendants had the option of having their charges dismissed, many were not taking that option. Many of those individuals took part in the county's drug court, which is an alternate to prison that focuses on treatment. This reluctance to drop their original case is a positive sign for the treatment program:

- Do the ends justify the means? In other words, was it worth having this bad situation to discover the following:
  - What a positive effect the drug court is having.
  - What ethical, concerned employees the laboratory has (in Hoover's colleagues).
- Do you think that this did indeed begin accidentally?
- How do you think this will affect his prior cases? What about current cases out of the laboratory?

Supporting a Habit (Huicochea, 2008)

The next example comes from the Tucson Police Department. Steve Skowron was a latent print examiner and a crime laboratory supervisor. Although he worked for the department for more than 20 years, he resigned after an investigation into missing drugs. Skowron was accused of mishandling six criminal cases between December 2004 and January 2006; methamphetamine, cocaine, and crack cocaine were missing from four of those cases. When Skowron was out of the laboratory, a coworker noticed that there were empty, unsealed packages of narcotics at Skowron's workstation. The department was not aware of mishandling until February 2008, when they learned of his personal consumption, but would not comment whether he had ever consumed drugs while on duty at the laboratory. The County Attorney's office planned to reopen 200 cases that Skowron had worked. At the time of the article, it was unclear if charges would be filed against Skowron or if all 200 cases would be reviewed by defense experts:

- If it were up to you, would you reopen or reexamine all of his cases?
- Could you explain a situation in which they may have just been a misunderstanding?
- If you were the County Attorney's office would you press charges?
- Do you think that the laboratory should give the latent print examiners (and other sections) the same type of scrutiny or standards that they give to the drug chemists?

"Errors" (Armstrong, 2007)

This example involves a forensic scientist who resigned from the Washington State Patrol. After finding three errors in cases he worked, the State Patrol underwent a review of Evan Thompson's work. The errors included incorrect analysis of a gunshot's trajectory, releasing information before having a supervisor review the work, and failing to identify a bullet's diameter. In his defense, the first case error passed peer and management review. Also, he released the information without review because it was needed immediately, and in some cases the diameter of the bullet was extraneous. Although the State Patrol had prior concerns with the quality of evidence handling and record keeping, Thompson stated that he was encouraged only to improve on his grammar and punctuation.

Thompson believes that he made conservative calls in his cases. If not 100% sure, he would not make a call. He passed every proficiency test in his career, always had matches peer reviewed, and was confident that no convictions based on his work would be overturned. When asked to comment on his resignation, Thompson said, "I've been in this business long enough to know that sometimes you can win the battle but lose the war" and that he was tired of a three-hour commute:

- What do you think came first—the three primary errors that were investigated or the "concerns" over the quality of Thompson's work? Why?
- In another part of the article, Thompson stated that he was "confident in his abilities." Do you think his actions support this statement? Why or why not?
- What are your overall thoughts on this example?

Prosecutor Pressure (Moxley, 2008)

Prosecutors asked the Orange County California Sheriff's Department crime laboratory to alter key exculpatory evidence, which led to the wrongful conviction of James Ochoa. The district attorney's office ignored exculpatory evidence in the case. The Orange County Sheriff's Department crime laboratory tests excluded Ochoa as a DNA contributor, even after two other scientists reviewed and verified the results. When the lead scientist, Danielle Wieland, told the prosecutors the results of the DNA tests, she was asked to lie to the defense council and tell them that Ochoa's DNA was found. After the district attorney's (DA's) office staff and the crime laboratory's staff went back and forth, the result was the scientists would not back down. Camille Hill, who is a veteran prosecutor and a former employee of the Houston crime laboratory, did not think that the requests from her office were abnormal. She said that the prosecutors often ask the crime laboratory to reconsider findings. Eventually, the DA's office accepted the findings.

Wieland, however, was never able to tell the jury about the evidence. Robert Fitzgerald, a Superior Court judge, confronted Ochoa without the jury present. He offered Ochoa a chance to plead guilty for a two-year sentence or continue the trial and face the possibility of life if found guilty. Ochoa took the deal out of fear. After spending 16 months in jail, DNA evidence was matched to the real perpetrator, and Ochoa was released by the DA, Tony Rackauckas. The DA's office is currently building its own DNA crime laboratory system independent of the current crime laboratory.

- How often do you think prosecutors pressure scientists?
- What future problems do you foresee with two contradicting crime laboratories in the same city?
- Would you have done anything differently if you were Wieland?
- Do you think Hill's background in forensic science has an effect on how she handled this particular case? If so, why?
- Do you think the title of the article, "CSI Games: If DNA Evidence Doesn't Fit in Orange County, Alter It?," is fair to the parties involved?

Detroit (Clickondetroit.com, 2008)

This example deals with an audit of the Detroit crime laboratory conducted by the Michigan State Police's firearms laboratory. In the report, it was shown that 1 of every 10 cases had serious mistakes in evidence evaluation. The Detroit Police Department's firearms laboratory met 42% of the 100% compliance with standards. The problems included human error, lack of funding, lack of resources, and improper training. Due to this finding, many appeals could be filed on past cases and hundreds to thousands of cases will need to be rereviewed. The Detroit police crime laboratory was temporarily closed in spring 2008 after errors were found from a double slaying case, but then the chief said he was "shutting the lab down." The Detroit mayor said that even with prior notification he was not ready for the amount of shocking and damning evidence that was provided by the report. Firearms evidence would be sent to one of the other Michigan State Laboratories for examination.

- The problems cited are not new to forensic laboratories; where do you think the Detroit lab went wrong?
- Do you think shutting down the laboratory was the correct way to go?

A follow-up by Moran and Gross (2008) contains details of the final report from the investigation into the Detroit Police Crime Laboratory. First, it was found that guns and bullets were unsecured and unprotected from contamination; records were missing in approximately 90% of the files, the scientific instrumentation was not properly calibrated, and many examiners were unqualified, if not completely untrained. The report also cited an error rate of greater than 10% in the 283 cases. Some of the cases also included assumptions about evidence that was not even tested. Due to this audit, the city is trying to secure funds to conduct a complete audit of all the crime laboratory sections.

The article lists some other recent ethical problems in crime laboratories in the United States:

- Houston Police Department's crime lab was shut down in 2003 for incompetence that affected thousands of cases.
- The Los Angeles Police Department fired a fingerprint analyst and suspended three others for false fingerprint identifications.
- A total of 13 technicians at the Federal Bureau of Investigation (FBI) crime laboratories had made serious errors and slanted testimony in 1997.

How do we handle this? To begin helping scientists and laboratories, funding and training need to increase, backlogs need to be reduced, and supervisors and managers need specialized training for management issues. Laboratories run by police agencies need to work toward independence so the laboratories are run by trained scientists, not police officers. This culture change will help to alleviate the "tunnel vision" of aiming for a conviction and replace it with the purpose of forensic science—to objectively state what the evidence shows. Evidence can provide reliable results when properly collected, stored, and tested by scrupulous scientists or investigators.

- What do you think is the best way to handle these issues?
- What was your reaction to the findings of the Detroit lab audit?
- Do you think the cultural differences between police and scientists are as much of a concern as this article and previous course content suggest? Why or why not?
- Do you think that an audit of all laboratory sections is feasible? How likely do you think it is to happen in Detroit?

Procedure (Johnson, 2008)

Barry Logan, a toxicologist since 1990 and a laboratory director since 1999, resigned on March 14, 2008. He oversaw eight laboratories for a total of 220 employees; staff and attorneys were shocked and saddened when they were told about the resignation. Logan is well known and respected in his field as he shows pride in the laboratories and takes responsibility for the errors, which in his opinion were overstated.

The resignation comes after a series of problems in the Washington State Patrol toxicology laboratory. The first issue occurred when a laboratory manager was accused of signing off on tests that she had not actually conducted. Logan received a vague tip regarding the wrongdoing and asked the manager in question to investigate the incident (it is thought that he was unaware that the person he asked to investigate the claim and the accused were the same person). The next issue involved the laboratory's procedure with breath-test machines. The employees maintain that inaccurate results are minimal although defense attorneys question the practices of the laboratory. Judges began to question Logan's credibility based on the errors occurring in the laboratory.

Although Logan had many supporters, he stated that he felt the laboratory would move forward better under a new director. One defense attorney believed that Logan wanted to run a laboratory based on integrity but failed to do so as many things went wrong under his management. The new director would hold a separate position from the state toxicologist, unlike how the position was structured in the past. Logan was responsible for both positions, which the State Patrol chief decided was "too much to ask of any one person."

- Do you think a resignation was necessary?
- Do you think Logan is the reason for the laboratories problems? If not, who is?
- How would you have handled the tip concerning the wrongdoing (which was ultimately one of Logan's mistakes)?
- What could have been done to prevent such drastic measures? On behalf of the laboratory? On behalf of Logan? On behalf of the staff? On behalf of the judges? On behalf of the attorneys?

Fingerprints (Associated Press, 2008)

After learning that police had arrested at least two innocent people based on erroneous fingerprint identifications, the Los Angeles Police Commission requested a review of the policies and procedures of the city's fingerprint analysis unit. Postinvestigation, reports cited a poorly run operation, shoddy work, a lack of oversight, and lost or misplaced evidence and records. It was shown that people were checking over their friends' work and at times, approving it without actually conducting a review. The department had 78 fingerprint analysts and two analysts that verify the results for accuracy. One fingerprint analyst was fired, three were suspended, and two supervisors in that section were replaced. Officials wanted to take quick action stating that "guilty people can be set free and innocent people can be jailed." Although they believed no one had been convicted of a crime based on identification mistakes, they would not know for sure without a full review. Officials had planned to hire an outside expert for an external review; however, they could not get the $325,000 to $450,000 in funding to pay for the review. This is a serious matter because, as one defense attorney stated, "Juries tend to afford the highest level of confidence to fingerprint evidence."

- How do you think the problem of funding the review should be handled?
- What if a full review cannot take place? Is this fair to the others who may have been convicted based on erroneous identifications?
- How sure do you think they are that "no one has been convicted of a crime based on identification mistakes"?
- Are you surprised that more people were not fired, demoted, or reprimanded?

Personal Gain (Bone, 2007)

This section deals with a forensic scientist who abused her authority and access for her own personal gain. Ann Chamberlain ran a DNA test on her husband's underwear in the crime laboratory, where she was employed since 1999, to determine if he was cheating. She then testified to conducting this investigation at the divorce hearing. The DNA test was discovered when her husband's lawyer sent a letter to her Michigan State Police laboratory questioning the improper DNA testing. Although Chamberlain had won awards for her work and testified in more than 50 cases, she was fired for misusing the crime laboratory.

Chamberlain stated that the tests were conducted outside of work hours with expired chemicals. It was later discovered through court testimony that she had previously conducted a paternity test for one of her husband's friends and had allowed him access to the laboratory while she ran his sample.

So where does everyone stand on the issue? The Michigan State Police suspended her with pay while conducting the investigation. After the investigation was completed, they fired Chamberlain for violating state policy. Her husband's lawyer felt that she should face criminal charges for stealing from taxpayers. The president of Forensic Science Consultants, where Chamberlain also worked, stated that she was an excellent scientist who made an error in judgment caused by stress and that it would not affect her position with the company.

- After hearing the different views of the issue, who do you most *agree* with? Why?
- After hearing the different views of the issue, who do you most *disagree* with? Why?
- Aside from abusing authority, what other ethical issues do you see with this case?

Research (Associated Press, 2006)

This example discusses scientists who personally accepted money from drug companies. The National Institutes of Health (NIH) started the investigation of 103 employees in 2004, after suspecting that many paid relationships with companies were going unreported. Through this investigation, NIH focused on 44 alleged offenders, many of whom left NIH voluntarily before any punishment could be enforced.

Only 2 of the 44 found to have violated rules regarding private consulting are being investigated for possible criminal activity. These two scientists were said to have committed such severe misconduct that, had they not been employed federally, they would have been fired immediately.

So What Happened?

Allegedly, human tissue samples were transferred from NIH patients to Pfizer inappropriately. Although the scientist denies that the consulting payments were related to things done in his governmental role, the consulting deals were unauthorized and did overlap with the governmental duties.

What Was the Scientists' Defense?

First, extremely long hours were worked in their government capacity, even if the correct procedures were not followed to request annual leave.

Second, NIH sent many mixed messages. They stopped the retirement proceedings of one of the scientists, they refused to meet with the scientist on the topic after having his cooperation, and they interfered with his research.

On the Other Hand...

A colleague, who had worked with NIH for 33 years, held nearly $2 million in stock with four different companies in which he was a board member while in his position at NIH. The consulting was approved, and he was never investigated for misconduct.

- Who is more right in this situation?
- Does the alleged "mistreatment" from the agency justify not going through the proper channels for permission?
- Is it fair that these two scientists were made into examples while many others were permitted to retire or leave the agency voluntarily before action was taken?
- Why do you suppose these scientists were singled out?
- Do you think there are details that would help you to make a judgment call on the case? If so, what are they?

FBI Whistle-Blower

In 2002, *Time Magazine* named three whistle-blowers as its "Persons of the Year." One of the women was Colleen Rowley, an FBI staff attorney who sent a memo to FBI director Robert Mueller about how the FBI ignored requests from a field office to investigate Zacarias Moussaoui, who is now indicted as a September 11 coconspirator. Although the attacks could not have been prevented, the FBI overlooked vital clues and withheld data. Rowley did the right thing simply by doing her job appropriately—with courage, honor, and intensity. She risked her job, her health, and her privacy. Initially, Rowley tried to deal with the problem in-house, but the details of her report were leaked to the public. She has a belief that the work her organization did was important and served a significant purpose. Confronting those at a higher pay grade came with severe repercussions. First, Cowley is the primary earner in her family. Next, if not fired, whistle-blowers are isolated and seen as extraneous. "There is a price to be paid," says Cynthia Cooper, another whistle-blower, who worked at World Com. Society needs to trust the integrity of federal institutions and to feel as though these institutions will act in society's best interest, especially in regards to terrorism. Rowley did not wait for others to do what she perceived as the right thing for the country; she took it on herself and faced the consequences and repercussions. However, when asked if she would do it again, her answer was negative.

All of the cases provided represent a perspective of each case. There are unknown details that allow the student of forensic ethics to ask questions and dig deeper. Not only do the cases provide ways that people may get into trouble, but they also open up the cases to further scrutiny.

Notorious Examples Every Forensic Scientist Should Know

Fred Zain

Fred Zain was a West Virginia scientist who began by claiming he had earned a master's degree that he did not actually possess. He later became notorious for providing incriminating testimony in capital murder cases without having done any analysis. After being fired in West Virginia, Zain was hired in a Texas forensic laboratory. Eventually he was convicted of fraud. (www.truthinjustice.org/expertslie.htm and www.corpus-delecti.com/forensic-fraud.html)

Michael West

Michael West was an odontologist from Mississippi who frequently testified that a particular weapon had *indeed and without doubt* caused a particular wound. After stating that he did not believe in reasonable scientific certainty as an appropriate standard, he proudly stated that his opinions were based simply on gut instinct. (www.reason.com/news/show/12167.html)

Kathleen Lundy

Kathleen Lundy, an employee from the FBI lab, admitted to "the adrenaline factor" too late and eventually pled guilty to making false statements. She was an expert on lead analysis of bullets and became upset at the frequency in which she was challenged in court by a former colleague. *The adrenaline factor* refers to the temptation of stating what was said beyond what is reasonably defended under cross-examination. (www.cbsnews.com/stones/2003/03/17/national/main544209shtml) (www.truthinjustice.org/FBI-crime-lab.htm and www.corpus-delecti.com/forensic-fraud.html)

Allison Lancaster

Allison Lancaster was a DNA analyst in a laboratory that required all staff to rotate weekends working drug cases. She was unhappy and angry so she wrote reports without doing analyses. She was caught because other analysts thought it was strange that no reagents were being used up after her working weekends. Lancaster was so upset with the laboratory and management that she took actions that would damage the reputation of the organization, without regarding the fact that it ultimately would have a more severe impact on her. (www.corpus-delecti.com/forensic-fraud.html)

David Petersen

In the case of former American Society of Crime Laboratory Directors (ASCLD) president and laboratory manager David Petersen, fear of discovery proved to be a powerful motivator for misbehavior. He was robbing one drug locker to repay another to avert the discovery of his initial misuse of drugs. (www.corpus-delecti.com/forensic-fraud.html)

Joyce Gilcrist

Joyce Gilcrist serves as an example of the pressures of a forensic scientist operating under the direct control of the police or operating as a forensic scientist who is also a sworn officer. Gilcrist was a hair examiner who received inadequate training and had no science mentor. She was popular with bosses and prosecutors because she always produced what for them was the *right* answer. She was convinced that she had never seen hairs from two individuals that she could not differentiate. (See above and "When Evidence Lies" Time.com by Belinda Luscombe, May 13, 2001 and www.corpus-delecti.com/forensic-fraud.html)

Houston Police Department Crime Laboratory

The review of the laboratory began after a contemptuous state audit of its work led to a suspension of genetic testing in January 2003. The audit found that technicians had misinterpreted data, were poorly trained, and kept substandard records. In most cases, the technicians used up all available evidence preventing defense experts from refuting or verifying the results. The laboratory's building was in poor shape, with a leaky roof that contaminated evidence. The problems in Houston are much greater than other crime laboratories in the United States because more defendants there have been executed than from any other area in the country. Police lab tailored tests to theories, report says by Roma Khanna, May 12, 2006, *Houston Chronicle*.

Codes of Ethics

8

Introduction

Codes of ethics are institutional guidelines used to reinforce ethical conduct. These codes are the written rules governing behavior based on moral values. They contain mandatory provisions and target guidelines that help to lessen the burden of gray areas. Codes are typically not detailed but instead are general in nature. Codes of ethics have two purposes. First, they provide moral guidelines and professional standards of conduct. The professional codes hold people accountable for proper performance and devotion to honesty and obligation. The second purpose of codes is to define professional behavior to promote a sense of pride, tolerance, and responsibility among professionals. The codes serve as a basis for disciplinary action and are regulated by laws of the legal and scientific communities. They are concerned with legal and moral behavior both personally and professionally. Typically, the personal aspects cover more than what is legally expected of members, such as personal morality, honesty, truthfulness, and virtue. Codes of ethics should dissuade people from acting unethically by providing general procedures, including the severity of and the consequences for unethical actions.

Some sources give the impression that, because there are so few established formal ethical codes, ethics are not generally considered important to forensic scientists, which is not the case. While having a code of ethics indicates the credibility and willingness of organizations to take responsibility, not having a code does not indicate irresponsibility of the profession. Many times the provisions set forth in a code of ethics are incorporated into codes of conduct of an agency or group. In this case, having a code of ethics is redundant although the group is still providing the guidelines in a different way. Some professions feel as though codes of ethics are worthless because they are vague and irrelevant. A common misconception regarding codes of ethics is that an action occurs frequently if it is addressed by a code. Though some codes state the perceived or previously encountered problems of a profession, those actions are not necessarily the most frequent. The codes are composed of general procedures and principles to maintain the quality of the profession based not only on past experience but also on actions that professions want to prevent altogether. In most cases, a person will receive support from an employer if he or she applies the code of ethics to a situation and the practitioner can justify the course of action. A reliance on ethical guidelines provides support for decisions that otherwise would be difficult to defend. Employees tend to find ethical management, the existence of codes of ethics, punishment for unethical behavior, and reinforcement for ethical behavior as the most important features of ethical professional cultures. Though they are necessary for professional practice, simply having codes is not sufficient to ensure that people will always take the "right" actions.

Support by the profession is important to maintaining codes of ethics. Support is gained when proper procedures are in place to maintain the effectiveness of the code. Proper procedures include methods for filing complaints, receiving complaints, investigating complaints, and reviewing complaints. The procedure for filing a complaint should be straightforward as to not intimidate the complainant but not too lenient so that people abuse the procedure to harass others. Mechanisms to decide if unethical behavior has occurred are important. The organization must decide how to weigh nonfactual matters such as statements of opinion or personal values. In addition, organizations should have procedures for hearings and appeals process. The solutions to problems must comply with the established standards of the profession and the organization. Groups should have a procedure in place to inform members of occurrences of unethical behavior. The claims and results of claims are important so members can adapt their methods accordingly. Though all of the major forensic science professional organizations employ codes of ethics, few ethical complaints are brought to the organizations.

An additional means of support for codes of ethics is record keeping. To review the qualitative aspects, an organization may develop an inventory of ethical problems. Such an inventory will help the organization to determine the variety and severity of occurrences. These records may also help the group to develop hypotheses about the causes and solutions to misconduct. Perhaps an organization would like to know the relative frequency of problems. Record keeping serves as a good judge as to where the profession is and where it needs to go regarding ethical conduct. Probably the most significant means of information tracking in forensic science is proficiency testing. Scientists are at times afraid to show their own levels of ability to the public; however, the tests are necessary to ensure the quality of the scientist and his or her agency as well as to remain open as part of the scientific culture.

Some scientists may not trust the proficiency of the scientists who are testing their results, but is it ethical to refuse a proficiency test? If so, is this proper professional conduct for forensic scientists?

National Forensic Center

The National Forensic Center has proposed a code of ethical conduct for forensic experts. The code, as described in Shiffman's (2000) *Ethics in Forensic Science and Medicine,* is in place to help experts recognize their social responsibility and to promote high moral and ethical standards. As with any code of ethics, the details are a guide, not a rulebook. The National Forensic Center is not a regulatory body, and compliance with the code is voluntary by experts. The code is divided into two parts: (1) the principles, which provide a framework for responsibility; and (2) the precepts, which are the standards for performance. It is the organization's goal to eventually add a portion for enforcement.

The *principles* are set forth so professional experts are mindful of their responsibilities and effect on the justice system. Public trust is the first responsibility because the actions of experts should serve and honor public interest. Experts are considered professional only when they employ a high standard of ethical commitment to the community and believe that their role is to serve the public. Dilemmas may stem from advocacy role of attorneys, vested interest of clients, and outside pressures; however, the experts who seek professional excellence and integrity after qualification as an expert are honoring their duty. The second responsibility of an expert is integrity. All aspects of professional responsibility must be performed with integrity. Not having specific rules regarding the relationship between experts and the adversary process necessitates experts to rely on their personal and professional integrity. The third responsibility of the expert is the objectivity and independence of decisions that are free from conflicts of interest. Experts advocate for their knowledge of the subject matter, not the client's cause. The next responsibility is professional care and competence for technical and ethical standards of the profession. Experts should exemplify competence in their role as an expert and as a teacher. The final responsibility for experts is an understanding of the scope and nature of their services. A person is an expert only on specific topics. He or she has a moral and social obligation to decline services that do not support the honest interpretation of facts. The background, qualifications, and professional records of experts should be kept current and made available for the triers-of-fact. Experts who assume these responsibilities maintain quality standards for performance.

The *precepts* section of the codes of ethics sets forth the experts' standards for performance. Personal standards include independence, integrity, and objectivity. The general practice standards clarify issues such as promotion and solicitation, background and qualifications, fee structure, professional cooperation, attorney–expert relationship, and personal publicity. The professional and technical standards are a guide for experts. Standards explain professional competence, due professional care, and significance of continuing education and training. The technical standards guide experts in methodology, professional criteria, and assuring that adequate data are available. The standards of presentation specifically relate to the role of the experts in court. Factors such as expert versus personal opinion, degrees of certainty, contents of written conclusions and opinions, form and impartiality of presentation, verification of conclusions, demonstrative evidence, discovery process, and differing opinions among opposing experts are included in the roles and responsibilities of expert witnesses. The final standard concerns experts' responsibility to fellow experts regarding integrity and opportunity. The National Forensic Center's code of ethical conduct provides a guide for professionals working in the adversary system.

Developing Codes of Ethics

The need for codes of ethics is recognized by most organizations, although many are modifying the development of codes so the resulting code is not too general. Fleckstein, Martone, and H. Pitluck (2001, p. 985) stated, "The absence of any statement on discrimination or harassment in almost two thirds of the policies seems to be a significant omission given the profile that these issues have at academic institutions and corporate centers." So how does a professional organization go about developing codes of ethics? First, the group must come to a mutual agreement regarding moral principles, the requirements of science pertaining to technology and information sharing, and legal requirements. The most challenging part about this process is coming to a consensus. Ideally, the development of the code must be a practice of the profession as a whole, not a result of the majority forcing its views on a minority. Groups must incorporate issues of personal morality along with specific ethical problems within the profession. During this process, the group should not exclude controversial issues as these issues are the most valuable experiences from which members can draw information. Codes should not get too specific; when this occurs, it excludes too many potential issues. It is important to remember that, when developing codes of ethics, more detailed codes are harder to revise. Developing a code of ethics requires a dedicated group of professionals that knows what type of code is required and what results it hopes to achieve. Four criteria that may help in the development process are that the code *must be desirable, feasible, enforceable,* and *enforced.* Codes should clearly demonstrate ideal goals as well as minimum conditions. The codes should be aimed at the everyday person, should be attainable, should be written in clear and specific language, and should progress in a logical order. Codes written so that they are applicable after decades are the most valuable. Results of the code include protecting the public's interest and the interests of those in the group. While general, the code should focus on the unique components of the group's functions, not simple guidelines like, "Do not steal." If written correctly, the codes should encourage discussion and reflection, should provide ethical guidance for the whole profession, and should make basic ethical values of the group clear. Organizations must create enforceable codes and should use the enforceability by taking action against challengers. Codes of ethics created by a wide variety of members, including all disciplines, will assure the appropriate standards for the field.

There are three types of codes. The first type of code is *general*, which provides little value as a guide in specific circumstances. It serves to supplement the codes of ethics for individual specialization areas, such as the American Academy of Forensic Sciences. The next type is *specific*, which helps to define a profession for the first time. This type bridges the gap between law, which has a strong ethical tradition, and science, which has tried to develop professional recognition and self-governance. An example of an existing specific code is the California Association of Criminalists' code. The final type is *personal*, which is used if no specific principles or rules are present. People must rely on their personal ethics for guidance. An example of this is an independently practicing forensic scientist who is not part of a scientific or law enforcement agency or professional organization. Personal codes influence the development, implementation, and support of more formal codes of ethics. Implementation of a code of ethics requires the knowledge, dedication, and compliance of the profession. Codes are effective only if they are explained and enforced. A forensic scientist should apply the fundamental standards of scientific ethics and personal integrity to benefit the profession and society. In corporate culture there may be a lack of policies or an abundance of bad examples used to shape an employee's ideal of truthfulness. Oftentimes, dishonesty is an indicator that policies are outdated. Codes of ethics require continual interpretation, revision, and amendments to aid in success.

Purpose

Now that the general meaning of *codes of ethics* has been stated, what is the purpose of using a code? First, codes guide the practitioner by acting as a ruler against which to measure actions. They provide a framework for members to use as a reference in more specific cases. They monitor, promote, and protect the profession by imparting standards. The codes are a method of maintaining harmony within professional organizations as they are used to adjudicate disputes among members. In 1982, John Jay College of Criminal

Justice founded the Institute for Criminal Justice Ethics to increase ethical standards, to inspire research, and to ensure ethical actions in criminal justice. The primary qualities with which the institute was concerned were the ethics of public service and the ethics of professionalism. The quality of *public service* includes such a responsibility to protect society that it overrules any connection with a particular group or individual. Those in public service are said to hold a higher moral character than the average person, which is not seen as a privilege as much as a virtue. *Professionalism* is striving toward excellence in a given field. It requires self-discipline, reasoning, maturity, rejection of private gain, and "being good" in general. The two approaches to professionalism are administrative and moral. Administrative concerns discipline, compliance, and organizational loyalty, while morality deals with the moral character of employees as well as managerial activities. The functions codes of ethics serve include educating new members, narrowing problem areas, potentially reducing the number of regulations imposed, providing a starting point for scrutiny over issues in the field, and setting forth rules for specific behaviors.

According to Peterson and Murdock (1989), codes of ethics serve three main purposes. First, the codes assure people outside of the profession that they can expect to receive a certain degree of uniformity in standards of performance and moral conduct from members. Next, the codes assure members within the profession that they can similarly rely on colleagues to maintain a certain level of technical and moral standards in exchange for conducting themselves in accordance with the same principles. Finally, the codes serve as a notice that people engaged in the profession, who are nonmembers of the association, are not bound to the code. The nonmembership may cause conduct of a lower order than of those within the organization. How successful are codes of ethics? At this point, there is no conclusive answer, but the following points may help in establishing an opinion:

- Codes that are taken seriously by professionals are meaningful to their work.
- The importance of successful codes must be acknowledged by administrators and supervisors.
- People must follow the standards set forth.
- A healthy organizational environment allows for codes effectiveness.

Think about the codes of ethics you follow. Do you think they are successful based on this criteria? Codes of ethics are important to professions and serve a very important function in forensic science.

Council of Scientific Society Presidents
Study of Codes of Ethics

In 1996, the Council of Scientific Society Presidents (CSSP) conducted a study funded by the National Science Foundation (NSF) on various codes of ethics. The CSSP is an organization of presidents, president-elects, and recent past presidents of 60 scientific federations and societies. The results showed the following:

- A total of 58% of professional organizations have written ethics policies.
- An additional 13% had draft policies under consideration.
- Only eight societies have designated a committee or official to investigate allegations of unethical conduct and have sanctions that are imposed if a member is found to act unethically.
- Policies vary in length from one sentence to 32 pages.
- There is a wide range of topics from traditional (privacy and confidentiality) to more recent (advertising for professional service).
- Most statements are one page or less.

Some groups did not want to employ codes of ethics to avoid lawsuits or because they expected other safeguards to take care of problems.

Familiarity with Codes of Ethics

Forensic scientists have a responsibility to become familiar with the written codes that govern scientific behavior. Scientists should understand how to apply the codes and should know how to reason beyond the explicit language. As of now, criminalist-specific codes of ethics do not exist; they are typically general statements. In fact, technically there is no standardized code of ethics for scientists in general. Scientists normally apply a code of ethics set by the institutions that employ them, funding agencies, or professional associations. Forensic scientists have a responsibility to understand the various codes to which they are held within their discipline, agency, and profession.

Here are some of the key points of major forensic professional organizations codes of ethics:

- Unbiased, rigidly impartial, logical, progressive.
- Adequate examinations; no bolstering of conclusions with unwarranted or superfluous tests.

- No unreliable, unproven, or discredited procedures.
- Maintain skills.
- No distortion of tests or interpretations.
- No confusion of scientific fact with investigative theory.
- No reporting beyond one's competence.
- Disclose exculpatory findings to the court, if necessary.
- No misrepresentation of qualifications.

As you can see, the codes generally contain provisions that fall into one of four areas. The areas are as follows:

1. The obligations to follow a scientific method in performing examinations and formulating conclusions.
2. The requirements concerning the impartial interpretation and presentation of laboratory results.
3. The behavior concerning courtroom demeanor and delivery of expert testimony.
4. The obligations to the profession as a whole and maintenance of one's own professional skills.

These provisions are the basis of ethical behavior in forensic science. No code of ethics could possibly deal with all of the intricate details of real situations; they merely serve as a guide.

The American Academy of Forensic Sciences (AAFS)

Article II. Code of Ethics and Conduct

SECTION 1 – THE CODE: As a means to promote the highest quality of professional and personal conduct of its members and affiliates, the following constitutes the Code of Ethics and Conduct which is endorsed by all members and affiliates of the American Academy of Forensic Sciences:

a. Every member and affiliate of the Academy shall refrain from exercising professional or personal conduct adverse to the best interests and objectives of the Academy. The objectives stated in the Preamble to these bylaws include: promoting education for and research in the forensic sciences, encouraging the study, improving the practice, elevating the standards and advancing the cause of the forensic sciences.

b. No member or affiliate of the Academy shall materially misrepresent his or her education, training, experience, area of expertise, or membership status within the Academy.

c. No member or affiliate of the Academy shall materially misrepresent data or scientific principles upon which his or her conclusion or professional opinion is based.

d. No member or affiliate of the Academy shall issue public statements that appear to represent the position of the Academy without specific authority first obtained from the Board of Directors.

SECTION 2 – MEMBER AND AFFILIATE LIABILITY: Any member or affiliate of the Academy who has violated any of the provisions of the Code of Ethics (Article II, Section 1) may be liable to censure, suspension or expulsion by action of the Board of Directors, as provided in Section 5h below.

SECTION 3 – INVESTIGATIVE BODY: There shall be constituted a standing Ethics Committee (see Article V for composition), the primary function of which shall be:

a. To order and/or conduct investigations and, as necessary, to serve as a hearing body concerning conduct of individual members or affiliates which may constitute a violation of the provisions of Article II, Section 1.

b. To act as an advisory body, rendering opinions on contemplated actions by individual members or affiliates in terms of the provisions of Article II, Section 1.

SECTION 4 – INVESTIGATION INITIATING ACTION: The following are the principal forms by which the Ethics Committee may initiate investigative action:

a. A member or affiliate of the Academy may submit a written complaint alleging violation(s) of Article II, Section 1 by a member or affiliate to the Academy Office (see Article II, Section 5, Rules and Procedures, below) or to the Chair of the Ethics Committee. Such a complaint should be made in a timely manner.

b. The Ethics Committee may institute an inquiry based on any evidence that may come to its attention from any source which in its opinion indicates the need for further query or action under the provisions of these bylaws.

SECTION 5 – RULES AND PROCEDURES: The following procedures shall apply to any allegation of unethical conduct against a member or affiliate of the Academy:

a. Allegations of unethical conduct against a member or affiliate received by the Academy shall be transmitted promptly to the Chair of the Ethics Committee.
b. The Ethics Committee shall determine whether the alleged unethical conduct falls within its jurisdiction and whether there is probable cause to believe that the allegation is well founded.
c. If the Ethics Committee, in its preliminary determination, finds that it does not have jurisdiction or that there is a lack of probable cause to believe that the allegation is well founded, it shall close the case. It shall issue a report of such determination to the Board of Directors, setting forth the basic facts but omitting the names of the parties, and stating the reasons for its decision to close the case. Notice of the allegation, including the source, and its disposition, shall be given to the accused. Notice of the disposition shall also be given to the complainant(s).
d. If the Ethics Committee finds that it has jurisdiction and that there is probable cause to believe that the allegation is well founded, it shall give notice of the filing of the allegation and its sources to the accused. In accordance with Rules and Procedures formulated by the Ethics Committee and approved by the Board of Directors, the Committee shall assemble such information from both the accused and the complainant(s) which shall permit it to determine whether the allegation requires further action.
e. The Ethics Committee may appoint an Academy Fellow or Fellows to investigate the allegation and/or to present the evidence to the Committee.
f. If, based on the results of an investigation, the Ethics Committee decides to dismiss the allegation without a formal hearing, it may do so. It shall notify the accused and the complainant(s) of its decision and shall issue a report to the Board of Directors setting forth the basic facts and stating the reason(s) for its decision, but omitting the names of the accused and complainant(s).
g. If the Ethics Committee decides to formally hear the case, it shall give the accused a reasonable opportunity to attend and be heard. The complainant(s) shall also be given a reasonable opportunity to be heard. Following the hearing, the Committee shall notify the accused and the complainant(s) of its decision. The Ethics Committee shall also submit a report on its decision to the Board of Directors. If the Committee finds unethical conduct, the report shall include the reasons for its decision, and any recommendations for further action by the Board.

The accused may also submit to the Board of Directors a written statement regarding what sanctions, if any, should be imposed.

h. If the Ethics Committee's decision is that unethical conduct on the part of the accused member or affiliate has occurred, the Board of Directors shall review the report, and ratify or overturn the decision, or remand the case to the Committee for further action. If the Board of Directors ratifies the Committee's decision, it shall also review any written submission provided by the member or affiliate found to be in violation of the Code. The member or affiliate may then, upon a vote of three-fourths of the members of the Board present and voting, be censured, suspended or expelled. The nature and conditions of any sanction must be provided to the member or affiliate. A suspended member or affiliate may only be reinstated by the procedure set forth in Article II, Section 6.

i. A member or affiliate who has been found in violation of the Code of Ethics has the right to appeal the actions of the Board of Directors to the membership of the Academy. To initiate an appeal, the member or affiliate must file a brief written notice of the appeal, together with a written statement, with the Academy Secretary not less than one hundred twenty days prior to the next Annual Meeting of the Academy.

j. The Board of Directors shall then prepare a written statement of the reasons for its actions and file the same with the Academy Secretary not less than forty days prior to the next annual meeting.

k. Within twenty days thereafter, the Academy Secretary shall mail to each voting member of the Academy a copy of the appellant's notice of appeal and supporting statement, and a copy of the Board of Directors' statement.

l. A vote of three-fourths of the members present and voting at the Academy's annual business meeting shall be required to overrule the action of the Board of Directors in regard to censure, suspension or expulsion of a member or affiliate.

m. No member of the Board of Directors who is the subject of an Ethics Committee investigation, or who has any other conflict of interest, shall participate in any matter before the Board concerning ethics.

n. The Ethics Committee shall formulate internal Rules and Procedures designed to facilitate the expeditious, fair, discreet, and impartial handling of all matters it considers. The Rules and Procedures shall be subject to the approval of the Board of Directors.

SECTION 6 – SUSPENSION OF MEMBERS AND AFFILIATES: Members or affiliates who have been suspended may apply to the Board of Directors for reinstatement once the period of suspension is completed. A suspended member or affiliate shall not be required to pay dues during the period of suspension. If reinstated, the required dues payment shall be the annual dues less the pro-rated amount for the period of suspension. (www.aafs.org)

The American Board of Criminalistics (ABC)

Rules of Professional Conduct

Article IV.5 of the By-laws of the ABC allows for disciplinary actions by the Board including denial and revocation of Certificates. Articles IV.5.1 through IV.5.3 state reasons for such action as follows:

1. An intentional misstatement or misrepresentation, or concealment or omission, of a material fact or facts in an application or any other communication to the Board or its representative(s).
2. Conviction of an applicant for certification or holder of a certificate by this Board by a court of competent jurisdiction of a felony or of any crime involving moral turpitude.
3. Issuance of a certificate contrary to or in violation of any of the laws, standard rules, or regulations governing the Board and its certification programs at the time of its issuance; or determination that the person certified was not in fact eligible to receive such certificate at the time of its issuance.

Article IV.5.4 also allows for disciplinary actions for the following reason:

4. Violations of the Rules of Professional Conduct of the ABC by an applicant or holder of a certificate of this Board.

The following are the Rules of Professional Conduct of the ABC, as referred to in Article IV.5.d, and together with Articles IV.5.1 through IV.5.3, they stipulate situations and rules which may, if violated, cause disciplinary action by the Board to be taken.

These rules describe conduct in the profession of forensic science (criminalistics) and are meant to encompass not only work done by Applicants, Affiliates, Fellows and Diplomates, but to the extent possible, work supervised by them as well. They meet general acceptance by peers in that profession. They specify conduct that must be followed in order to apply for, receive, and maintain the certification status provided for by the American Board of Criminalistics.

Applicants, Affiliates, Fellows and Diplomates of the ABC shall:

1. Comply with the By-laws and regulations of the ABC.
2. Treat all information from an agency or client with the confidentiality required.
3. Treat any object or item of potential evidential value with the care and control necessary to ensure its integrity. ABC 500, 12/07 Page 2 of 2
4. Ensure that all probative exhibits in a case receive appropriate technical analysis.
5. Ensure that appropriate standards and controls to conduct examinations and analyses are utilized.
6. Ensure that techniques and methods which are known to be inaccurate and/or unreliable are not utilized.
7. Ensure that a full and complete disclosure of the findings is made to the submitting agency.
8. Ensure that work notes on all items, examinations, results and findings are made at the time that they are done, and appropriately preserved.
9. Render opinions and conclusions strictly in accordance with the evidence in the case (hypothetical or real) and only to the extent justified by that evidence.
10. Testify in a clear, straightforward manner and refuse to extend themselves beyond their field of competence, phrasing their testimony in such a manner so that the results are not misinterpreted.
11. Not exaggerate, embellish or otherwise misrepresent qualifications, when testifying.
12. Consent to, if it is requested and allowed, interviews with counsel for both sides prior to trial.
13. Make efforts to inform the court of the nature and implications of pertinent evidence if reasonably assured that this information will not be disclosed to the court.
14. Maintain an attitude of independence and impartiality in order to ensure an unbiased analysis of the evidence.
15. Carry out the duties of the profession in such a manner so as to inspire the confidence of the public.
16. Regard and respect their peers with the same standards that they hold for themselves.
17. Set a reasonable fee for services if it is appropriate to do so, however, no services shall ever be rendered on a contingency fee basis.
18. Find it appropriate to report to the Board any violation of these Rules of Professional Conduct by another Applicant, Affiliate, Fellow or Diplomate. (www.criminalists.com)

American Society of Crime Laboratory Directors

Prior to developing a code of ethics, some people within ASCLD opposed guidelines and thought that it was better to leave issues of ethics to regional associations. The decision was made to disregard this stance because the positives far outweighed the negatives. Some of the things that a code helps with are checking and verifying credentials and training, protecting members from external pressures, overseeing testimony of scientists, assuring reports are supported by laboratory documentation, assuring that reports and testimony balance the data, and assisting with professional conflicts.

The ASCLD code of ethics deals with the various professional responsibilities of forensic scientists, particularly laboratory directors. The responsibility as an employer is to pursue the goals of the parent organization. The responsibility to employees is to foster internal relationships; to supervise and manage the working environment; to provide education, training, and professional development; and to maintain objectivity and not succumb to influences by adversaries. The employer is also responsible for hiring people with the necessary amount of training, skills, and proficiency and setting realistic performance goals for employees. The laboratory director has a responsibility of public interest to avoid activities that interfere with his or her independent judgment. The responsibilities to the profession include supporting employees in professional activities and societies; supporting academic programs, interns, and research; and supporting accreditation. It is recommended that the code include a section on quality assurance to verify and monitor proficiency of investigations and the courtroom activities of analysts. Though there was hesitation in the beginning, ASCLD's code of ethics has served as a model for many other organizations. Because there are written, validated procedures in place that assure legitimacy and objectivity of work performed, the code provides guidance on the proper scientific working environment and shows commitment to achieving goals. The code also encourages employees to participate in activities of professional societies. The responsibilities spelled out by ASCLD's code of ethics serve as a guide for laboratory directors and many other organizations that seek the same professional structure. (www.ascld.org)

The International Association for Identification (IAI)

- "As a member of the International Association for Identification, and being actively engaged in the profession of Scientific Identification and Investigation, I dedicate myself to the efficient and scientific administration thereof in the interest of Justice and the betterment of Law Enforcement."

- "To cooperate with others of the profession, promote improvement through research, and disseminate such advancement in my effort to make more effective the analysis of the expert."
- "To employ my technical knowledge factually, with zeal and determination, to protect the ethical standards of the profession of Scientific Identification and Investigation."
- "I humbly accept my responsibility to Public Trust and seek Divine guidance that I may keep inviolate the Profession of Law Enforcement."

Additional codes of ethics, including those used by law enforcement and international forensic organizations, are located in Appendixes B-D. (www.theiai.org)

An Ethical Approach to Forensic Professionalism

9

The concept that we are all human and capable of making mistakes.... that is not unethical.... What you do when a mistake is uncovered is the ethical part....

Source unknown

Introduction

Forensic science is a diverse profession that commonly interacts with many other high-profile professions. In exploring the various pressures associated with forensic science, law enforcement, and the judicial system one can appreciate how professionals might experience professional turmoil. The pressures associated with each profession are multiplied when the interaction of those cultures is considered. Now that we have discussed the interactions between professions and potential problems, how do we use this knowledge to prevent future issues? Knowledge, open minds, awareness, professionalism, and education are a good start. Although those of you reading this may have the highest personal and professional morals and ethical perspectives, you are now equipped with the knowledge necessary to observe those around you. It is quite possible, and hopeful, that you will take a closer look at colleagues and question their actions, motivations, and perspectives. The observation may cause empathy for their perspective or create more questions. This chapter explores the options for building a solid ethical future for forensic science.

Education

Forensic science has a few guiding principles for the profession. First, forensic scientists should have technical competence and employ reliable methods of analysis. Second, scientists should maintain honesty with respect to qualifications and should confine examinations to their areas of expertise. Next, scientists should partake in intellectual honesty concerning the scientific data on which their conclusions and opinions are based. Finally, objectivity in the review of evidence and the delivery of expert testimony is a principle of forensic science. The delivery of expert testimony refers to assuring the information is understandable to nonscientific fact finders. These guiding principles are the basics of ethics in forensic science, but how do we provide all forensic scientists with this understanding of the profession? In a word, *education.*

Ethics is a difficult subject to teach, which is why historically there has been a perceived lack of ethics training in forensic science. There is a debate about how and where to teach ethics. Ethics has been taught informally by example or through the use of examples from "the real world" in the past, so why change the passive, informal, implicit instruction? Science is now larger, faster, more complex, more expensive; is under the scrutiny of government, media, and society; and consists of greater pressures to publish and to obtain funding. Recently, higher education forensic science programs cover ethical issues in a variety of courses as an underlying theme of forensics. When college students are asked if they have had an ethics course (or even a lecture dedicated to the topic), most respond that they have not. Colleges and universities are equipping students with information on the ethics in the practice of forensic science; however, the students do not realize the value of the lessons they are taught until they need to apply the lessons to real-world situations. In the discussion of ethics in higher education, one must consider some additional questions. Is it the responsibility of high schools to teach ethics? Do ethics undermine, support, or stay indifferent to religion? How should ethics be taught? Who should teach ethics? Should ethics be covered in undergraduate programs or only in master's programs? Why should people take an ethics class if they have learned ethics throughout their life? Should laboratories assure that all employees receive ethics training upon hire? Should agencies be required to update employees every so often? *What do you think?*

Currently there are steps toward a decision regarding how and where to teach ethics in forensic science. There is a uniform curriculum provided by the Forensic Science Educational Program Accreditation Commission (FEPAC) for all college-level academic programs in forensic science. Ethics is a required part of accredited degree programs. In addition, Scientific Working Groups (SWGs) provide guidelines and certification programs. The working groups establish training, validation, and interpretation of standards. These groups indicate that the profession is interested in creating and maintaining good scientific practices. Recently, American Society of Crime Laboratory Directors-Laboratory Accreditation Board (ASCLD-LAB) has begun requiring laboratories seeking accreditation to assure that new laboratory employees have a minimum amount of ethics training. Currently, the major objections to teaching ethics are that professional ethics are best taught within the profession and that it is impossible to teach ethics because people are either moral or not. To the first point, how can we assure that the subject is taught and taught well through informal on-the-job training? To the second point, it is correct that a class cannot change an inherently unethical person; however, the concepts of personal ethics and professional ethics differ. Ethics classes do not seek to teach right from wrong; information is provided regarding the importance of ethical conduct and potential areas of conflict to facilitate advanced knowledge of the subject. Ethics courses are not intended to make a person ethical as much as they strive to provide a foundation to expand people's perspectives, to assist in maintaining open minds, and to create awareness. It seems that refresher courses have an effect on people, even if it is subconscious. Dan Ariely (2008), who teaches behavioral economics at Massachusetts Institute of Technology (MIT), discusses the surprising effectiveness of honor codes in schools and in workplaces in his book *Predictably Irrational*:

> It does seem more effective if people are reminded of their ethical responsibilities on a regular basis—even if they're ethical people, the reminder serves as a booster. Annual refresher training would be a useful addition to professional meetings or in-service classes.

Guidelines for education in forensic ethics include reading, writing, and discussing the topic. Education on ethics should encourage the acceptance of uncertainty while fostering the responsibility for a questioning attitude. The goal of teaching ethics is to shape human conduct through the ability to observe the "big picture." Those who teach ethics need to promote informal learning by acting as role models and mentors and through casual discussions with students. A high-quality ethics course teaches students awareness of the types of errors, sources for errors, and the importance of avoiding errors. Requirements for specific and appropriate education are necessary to standardize curriculum of ethics courses. Standardization of content is difficult because of a lack of funding, the widespread physical location of scientists, and the range of experience level or discipline focuses. In the past, scientists have become *forensic* scientists as a response to a need in the field and a lack of formalized training. With the development of academic programs in forensic science at the college level and the Forensic Educational Program Accreditation Commission (FEPAC), ethics courses in forensic science are becoming part of the regular curriculum. Ethics courses are implemented because codes of ethics are general in nature, the proper cause of action is not always obvious in every situation, or not all professional standards are appropriate in every situation. It is important to remember that a course in ethics will not provide answers to dilemmas or provide the correct answers for situations; however, ethics courses should provide people with the tools to question, evaluate, and discuss situations and possible outcomes.

What are the necessary points to cover in a forensic ethics course? The three core values in teaching ethics are integrity, innovation, and commitment. Course materials should contain a balance of case studies, theory, and methods. Students should learn official codes of ethics, terminology, and the key concepts in the profession. It is important for instructors to present a range of values beyond their own, just as exposure to differing views is necessary for students. As instructors develop ethics courses, they should consider what texts to use, what additional resources are available, and what copyright information is necessary. Textbooks, published articles, computer programs, Web pages, and video recordings are excellent means of providing information. Any new knowledge is useful for stimulating thoughts and creativity that encourage people to make changes and prevent future problems. The goal of ethics courses is to provide students with the skills to identify, articulate, and resolve ethical problems. Courses should increase students' understanding of underlying moral and ethical principles, should help develop students' ability to analyze problem situations and make decisions, and should encourage the development of skills and confidence to resolve ethical problems. The requirements provide an outline of the important aspects of a course on forensic ethics.

Competence

Forensic scientists and related professionals have varied training and experience regarding ethics that is not always based on formal education. Current trends in education affect how society views the competence of forensic scientists. Competence of expert witnesses is determined by a judge, who decides if a scientist qualifies as an expert, or the jury, which decides if the expert's testimony is reliable. The topic of competency has gained importance among professionals as well as academicians regarding scientific integrity. For example, are unethical actions taken because a person intends to deceive or because he or she simply does not know any better? The scientific community has a responsibility to society to address such issues for the profession to maintain the highest possible integrity. Society will have a better idea of how things have gone wrong in the past, how to prevent future problems, and how to change the overall course of unethical behavior. The accountability shown by the scientific community demonstrates that although no profession is perfect, at least the field of forensic science has safeguards in place and is forward thinking in regards to proper behavior and procedures.

Credibility of forensic scientists depends on the reliability and accuracy of the work performed. It is often difficult for laypersons to believe that forensic scientists remain objective based on the nature of the cases in which they work. For instance, can a forensic scientist remain impartial when investigating a child molestation case? Some people believe that the scientist should have no details of a case, whereas others think that the details are necessary for examinations.

What do you think? Do you think that this is different for every scientist? Do you think that this is different for the various disciplines in forensic science?

Forensic scientists do not make evidence "objective" through analysis; bias may have been applied in collecting evidence in the field. Scientists cannot completely control the process but can assure that personnel are properly trained. There is a great deal of pressure for scientists to remain accurate, efficient, and as forthright as possible. Many cases of ethics are not about what is right or wrong as much as they are about which choice is better or worse. Unlike science, ethics is a subjective discipline that creates issues that are hard to prove "beyond a reasonable doubt." Due to the subjective nature of ethics, people often question the credibility of professionals who are involved in investigating misconduct.

Professions and Professionalism

Acceptable behavior is defined within the various professional groups in which we participate, whether a laboratory, agency, professional association, committee, or business. Each group has a code of acceptable behavior known as professional ethics. Professions are complex social organizations that evolve over time and define themselves. Members agree on internal codes of practice and establish the relationship between the profession and the rest of society. Codes of practice include training, education, certification, licensure, and code of ethics. If members share a moral ideal, they represent the core values of the profession. There are some stereotypes regarding professional ethics. People tend to think that professionalism implies setting aside personal ideas to focus solely on the profession and also that professional ethics are summed up in the code of ethics without attention to the individual's ideals, virtues, or character. Individuals are shaped by their environment, politics, religion, culture, and families; these factors require consideration. Professional ethics are unattainable without a sense of individual morality; however, just because someone exhibits virtues in their professional life does not mean he or she does the same in his or her personal life (or vice versa). Adolf Hitler's scientists were a good example of this; they were considered nice people personally, but they were evil professionally. The final aspect to consider regarding professions is the leadership role. Leadership describes exerting influence from a position of authority, fostering cooperation, and persuading a group toward particular actions. Ineffective leadership occurs when there is incompetence, callousness, corruption, disregard for people, and a lack of self-control. More specifically, leaders who are greedy, disloyal, or selfish are not useful for professions. Proficient leaders advance professions because they take effective and ethical actions. Professions are large groups that combine personal characteristics and excellent leadership to create standards of appropriate behavior for its members.

Standards of behavior are a starting point to ensure ethical behavior and integrity within the forensic science profession. In addition to standards, practitioners should seek to advance the future of the profession through the creation of environments that promote ethical behaviors, the discovery of fresh possibilities as opposed to traditional ones, and redefinition of professional roles, if necessary. Ethics starts with each of us; it is important to embrace diversity and the varying thoughts or opinions that create individuals. It is important to talk about ethics, to ask questions, to keep searching for answers, to encourage ethical behavior, and to discourage unethical behavior. People should review situations to determine who benefited, who did not benefit, why it took a particular direction, and how it could have ended differently. Creativity is a useful tool in advancing the study of ethics because it involves curiosity, open-mindedness, flexibility, perseverance, purpose, experimentation, and patience. These characteristics help individuals to produce valuable new ways of thinking and approaching situations. The advancement of ethics depends on individual awareness.

Awareness

Why should people take preventive measures against unethical conduct? Recently the public has been increasingly interested in the importance of ethical conduct. The focus is a direct result of individuals and corporations such as Enron, WorldCom, Arthur Andersen, Martha Stewart Omnimedia, and Bernie Madoff that have endured large, highly publicized ethical scandals. These examples have heightened the public's awareness of misconduct; so now what measures will improve society's overall outlook on ethics? The first step to improving ethical behavior is awareness—a clear picture of the current state of ethics is needed before professions can plan for the future. Awareness encourages practitioners to take greater care in responding to ethical concerns when they arise. Support from scientific and professional literature is vital to increase ethical awareness in forensic science. Although not universal, many of the corresponding professions encounter similar ethical pressures and dilemmas to forensic science. It is important to realize that even small-scale ethical issues are serious because these actions have the potential to lead to even bigger problems. Increased communication among professionals regarding solutions to common dilemmas will improve ethical practices. If the fundamental standards of science and personal integrity are applied to dilemmas, ethical debates are minimized to the betterment of the profession and of society.

It is important to consider many possible solutions to ethical dilemmas and to consider society as a whole rather than individual or organizational interests. The practice of ethics is advanced by overcoming ignorance, embracing uncertainty, reporting results honestly, and, most importantly, recognizing the responsibility of forensic scientists. Openness and awareness are the first steps in creating a more ethical discipline.

Once professions become aware of the ethical issues common to the field and before they begin to change such practices, discussions should take place. Language is a crucial factor in the communication of ethical issues. Communication affects the impact of an issue and also influences the stance a person will take on the issue. The language used may manipulate a person's viewpoint if the words chosen exaggerate points. This type of communication is known as *loaded language* and is eliminated with the use of neutral, descriptive words. Another common problem in communication of ethical matters is ambiguous terminology. To alleviate this problem, one should attempt to clarify words or phrases that people could easily misunderstand. Although definitions contribute to clarity, an additional explanation is commonly required, such as during court testimony. Forensic scientists should not talk down to juries but should provide an explanation that will improve jury members' overall knowledge of the subject matter. Ways to enhance communication concerning ethical matters include listening carefully, respecting alternate views, having a willingness to learn, and actively participating in the conversation by asking questions, speaking calmly, seeking common ground, and remaining engaged. Actions to avoid in conversations about ethics are monopolizing the conversation, speaking loudly, exaggerating differences, exploiting weaknesses, and using facts only as weapons. One should avoid these actions because they are ineffective, do not contribute to new ideas, and prevent trust from the other party. The goal of communicating ethical issues is to inform people, to negotiate the outcome, or to gain further perspective on the issue.

National Academy of Sciences Report

In February 2009, the National Academy of Science published *Strengthening Forensic Science in the United States: A Path Forward*, in which recommendations were made to improve the current practices throughout forensic science. Topics include integrated governance, admissibility issues regarding forensic evidence, education and training, Automated Fingerprint Identification Systems (AFIS), Homeland Security, methods and practices, and strengthening the oversight of forensic science practices. The oversight of practices looks at accreditation, quality control, proficiency testing, certification, and codes of ethics. The publication states that "a uniform code of ethics should be in place across all forensic organizations to which forensic practitioners and laboratories should adhere" (p. 214). The National Academy of Sciences formally recommends the following:

> The National Institute of Forensic Science (NIFS), in consultation with its advisory board, should establish a national code of ethics for all forensic science disciplines and encourage individual societies to incorporate this national code as part of their professional code of ethics. Additionally, NIFS should explore mechanisms of enforcement for those forensic scientists who commit serious ethical violations. Such a code could be enforced through a certification process for forensic scientists (p. 26).

Based on this recommendation, the forensic science profession could potentially face major changes. Although there are benefits as well as drawbacks to implementing a national, uniform code of ethics, ultimately it will benefit the profession. Such a code could lessen the gray area while it creates a uniform mechanism with which to arbitrate misconduct. The report has the ability to greatly impact the forensic science profession if recommendations are used.

Some people will now hesitate when the natural human reaction is to judge a situation based on their personal morals, while other people will assure that many questions are asked before making accusations of someone for unethical behavior. It is important to ask questions in all situations and to create your own ethical judgment based upon these simple questions: Do you agree or disagree with what occurs? If there is disagreement, what compromises are available? What is the gravity of the situation, the circumstances, and the consequences? Hopefully this information has expanded your awareness, will allow you to observe situations more openly, and will encourage you to ask more questions. Forensic science is an ethical professional culture that operates in conjunction with legal and criminal justice professional cultures; the relationships and roles differ but do not need to divide the professions.

Appendix A: Initial Research Data on Ethics in Forensic Science

The initial research on ethics began after conducting a survey at the 2006 American Academy of Forensic Sciences annual meeting. Responses were provided by a variety of forensic professionals; experience levels, disciplines, and agency affiliations were represented by the 600-plus pieces of data collected. The statistics and a collection of specific responses to the most pertinent questions are provided. With the vast amount of data, text responses will be limited to a select few that represent the information as a whole. The material is being presented for educational purposes—it is not the intention of the author to pass judgment on the responses provided; however, readers are encouraged to consider the implication of some responses.

Question 1: In your opinion, how important is ethics to forensic science?

Very Important: 90%
Important: 8%
Somewhat Important: 1%
Not Important: < 1%

Question 2: When asked to rate some of the top ethical concerns of forensic science, professionals ranked them as follows:

Falsification of Data: 24%
Lying: 21%
Omitting Evidence: 14%
Pressured Testimony: 10%
Misrepresenting Credentials: 9%
Plagiarizing: 8%
Silence: 6%
Misuse of Resources: 4%
Padding Travel Expenses: 2%
Misuse of Sick Days: 2%

**Question 3: Do you think forensic scientists
receive adequate training in ethics?**

*No: 68%
Yes: 28%
Don't Know: 4%

*Upon stating that forensic scientists do not receive adequate training in ethics, professionals provided the following explanations (These statements are taken directly from an anonymous survey of forensic professionals.):

- Not aware of any formal available training.
- In many programs there are no forensic science ethics courses, and medical ethics are often hard to get into.
- Not at the educational level, because the number of trivial general education requirements does not allow for schedule flexibility.
- Ethical person usually goes on in forensic science.
- Very few formal opportunities.
- Supervisors don't always enforce ethic codes.
- I think that people are naive. They think everyone is ethical so don't spend as much time educating on ethics.
- It's just assumed that the scientist possesses sound ethics.
- Not everyone has the same ideas of what is "okay."
- Need to be willing to stand up against big egos because it can be the right thing to do, no matter how difficult.
- It depends on your discipline.
- Can't teach honesty.
- Because I see too much unethical behavior.
- I believe ethics is something you learn growing up. A course through work is probably inadequate at teaching ethics.
- Cost; ignorance.
- Assumption that there are no external factors that rearrange priorities for the scientist (e.g., alcohol problem, gambling, extreme debt).
- They don't take it seriously.
- Most funds are directed to "hands-on" education.
- I regularly discuss ethical problems with my trainees. I doubt they would recognize they have had ethics training.
- The expectations of the courts are changing.
- People don't understand the importance.
- Unfortunately ethics is not something that can be learned. You either are an ethical person or you're not.
- Inadequate teachers and no penalties for ethical violators.

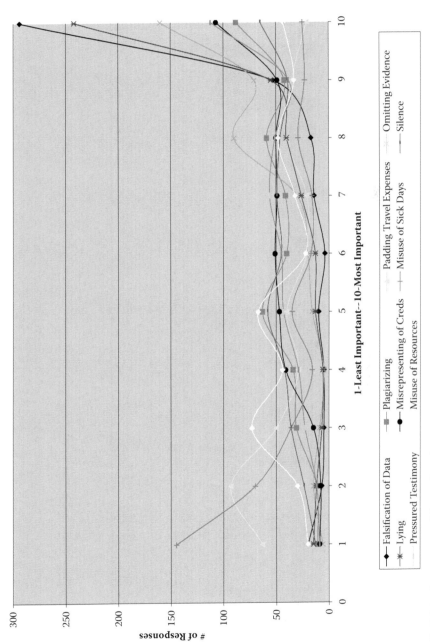

Figure A.1 Ethical concerns of forensic science.

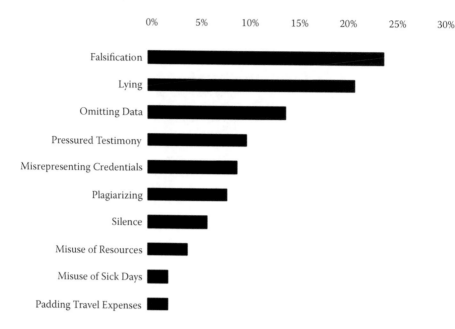

Figure A.2 Ethical concerns in order.

Question 4: Should all forensic scientists be required to follow the same ethical guidelines?

Yes: 89%
No: 11%

Points to consider:

- Ethics are cultural. Each culture should decide its own ethics.
- Different fields and techniques.
- Can require all you want; ethics will be individual.
- Everyone has his or her own opinion.
- Some should be the same; some are specific to position.
- Limits of information or common methods impinge on absolutes.
- Certain basic ethics are one's own personal makeup and cannot be taught.
- Private sector has differences.
- Depends if local agency has special requirements.
- For the most part I would say yes, but some disciplines (e.g., medicine) do have different constraints regarding things such as confidentiality.
- I don't believe it is possible for all people to follow the same ethical guidelines.
- Some fields have unique ethical concerns.

- Who will be the ethics police? Who decides what is and isn't ethical? Very dangerous and slippery slope.
- Variety improves coverage.
- Often depends on the situation, the details, the issues.
- Qualifications, no. All should have the same general ethics training, but some disciplines will require specific training in situational ethics.

Question 5: Are there specific examples of unethical behavior that you can share?

- Professional (pathologist) telling lies or gossip about another doctor.
- Personal relationships with the boss lead to unwarranted praised and promotions.
- Prosecutor had confession of shooting, but when he was told that didn't match autopsy findings, he did not have autopsy testimony and instead took quick and easy plea bargain based on confession.
- Working outside area of expertise or training and not knowing pitfalls.
- Yes, one incident of a person lying several times. I documented it, and she was fired.
- Coworker claimed overtime for work on a personal paper for which he receives money. I called him in my office, changed his time card, and took away overtime right.
- Working in autopsy with persons who are well acquainted with decedents.
- A tech in my lab purposely omitted negative control so quantity of DNA would never fail based on negative control failing.
- I had a district attorney try to get me to testify to something that was beyond the science—to oversimplify because he did not understand the concepts.
- A lot of experts lie about credentials. One of my peers says he is an engineer—no professional engineer's (PE) license—and says he did a thesis he did not.
- Concern for senior scientists who put themselves as only author on awards or publications and completely ignore recognizing any contributions from graduate students.
- Cheating on a proficiency test.
- False testimony.
- Pressure from officers to give conclusions not scientifically founded. Other labs then gave the desired conclusion for a price.
- Professors badmouthing colleagues to students, not giving enough direction to graduate students, not sending reference letters on

time. My experience mostly involves a certain university. I think the professors don't take their obligations seriously.

- Mishandled evidence once admitted and testified to on stand. Sometimes pressure to "produce statistics"—although I haven't, there is great potential to allow quality to suffer.
- One knows that someone has been paid to testify in a matter that is obviously false.
- Ranked their 3 answers. 1.) Falsification of data 2.) overestimating credentials 3.) offering opinion outside of discipline.
- My supervisor had to report her boss for unethical behavior and she did not.
- Abuse of overtime. I work with sworn officers who qualify for overtime, while I do not. I've witnessed abuse of overtime and brought it up to supervisor, but nothing was done. This becomes a demotivating factor for retention.
- Falsification of data (notes) discovered during peer review process; falsifying peer review documents to get docs through quickly; scientists reporting on work they had others do (reported as their own work).
- Superior allowed one employee to "borrow" a case of Xerox paper while formally charged another for theft of government property (fuel in the amount of $10) and official misconduct. First employee never replaced the paper worth $50. Inconsistent in ethical code.
- Falsifying timesheets.
- Falsifying data.
- Pressured testimony (by state's attorney).
- Using agency resources for personal gains.
- Evidence planted by crime scene processors.
- One employee "resigned" for misrepresentation of American Academy of Forensic Sciences (AAFS) membership. One employee "resigned" for misrepresentation of academic credentials.
- Critical attempt to destroy the competence of another expert in an unethical manner.
- Sharing of information that is supposed to be kept confidential—people don't seem to take it seriously.
- Extensive coaching of certain individuals prior to inspections to ensure they pass.
- I am aware of an individual who has applied to the AAFS, and I am actively working to block acceptance since I believe he has violated AAFS ethical policy.
- Yes, multiple, but I can't share them without risk of retaliation.
- One colleague lied about another's credentials or training to divert the incoming casework to his own lab.

Question 6: Respond to the following scenario.

You drive to a professional meeting with a colleague in your personal vehicle. When you return, you submit a travel voucher for your expenses, including mileage. As you turn in your form, you notice your colleague's travel voucher also requests reimbursement for mileage, even though you drove. What should you do?

- Bring it to the colleague's attention—may be a simple oversight. If it continues then bring it to attention of supervisor.
- I probably should tell someone, but honestly I would not because the company should investigate and it is not worth the trouble between coworkers.
- I am not responsible for other people if they choose to lie; it's on them.
- Make him buy you lunch.
- Never take the lying bastard to another meeting.
- Nothing.
- Speak up; stealing is stealing.
- Discuss with colleague. This is a personal ethics matter, not a scientific ethics matter.
- Who cares?
- Talk to my colleague and try to get them to withdraw mileage request. I would not tell my boss.
- Blatant violation of county policy; therefore legally it must be addressed. It has nothing to do with ethics in this case.
- Stop looking at confidential papers.
- Worry about more substantial issues.

Question 7: Respond to the following scenario.

You arrive at the location of the crime scene to discover that it is the house of someone with whom you have a long history of disputes. Is it ethical for you to continue on the case?

- No (the majority of the answers).
- Yes.
- No; it is not ethical for me to continue until or unless I explain my conflict of interest to my supervisor.
- I would excuse myself from the case mainly to avoid appearance of impropriety.
- Depends on what your role in the investigation is. If you are just collecting evidence there's not as much conflict of interest as if you were an interrogator.

- Yes, as long as I can separate the personal issue and not let it affect my judgment.
- Yes, ethical.
- Absolutely not!
- Depends on issue.
- Probably not, but may be difficult to get other coverage in our system.

Suppose it's not you but a colleague who has a bad history with the owner; he told you this in confidence. Should you tell your supervisor?

- Yes (majority answer).
- As a professional it shouldn't matter, but yes, because it could cause problems in court.
- It depends whether there is anyone else to substitute. It would be better not to.
- Encourage colleague to step down his participation or disclose information to his supervisor. Volunteer to perform duties that involve direct interaction with homeowner to lessen any substance or detrimental methods.
- I would hope my colleague could still process the scene professionally regardless of my personal feelings for someone. I would probably let the detective know, but it wouldn't affect my judgment in processing the scene or evidence.
- No; you will be guided by your ethical principles in the investigation.
- Depends—homicide or burglary? Importance of case makes a difference.
- The conflict isn't between the two of you—if you can remember that what you hear from the colleague is one-sided and take into account your coworker's personality. Take all stories and conflicts with a grain of salt.
- Absolutely. The colleague could be accused of misconduct.
- Yes; the integrity of processing the crime scene could be questioned without full disclosure.
- It is not ethical for you to work in either case.
- I wouldn't tell my supervisor.

Question 8: Do you have any formal ethics training?

- No (majority answer).
- Medical school.
- Some—we take a four-hour class I think every other year. We also have a booklet (if it's read).
- B.S., B.A.—philosophy

- Yes, required as part of law degree.
- Two courses (responsible skills and conduct in scientific research).
- Yes, ethics class and section of class specific to forensic science ethics.
- Yes, through master of forensic science program.
- Course taken in police academy.
- Yes; U.S. Army requires all lab personnel to attend annual ethics training. Also I have served as chair professional conduct committee for a regional forensic organization (SWAFS).
- Yes, provided by agency (not forensic specific).
- AAFS and International Association for Identification (IAI) workshops.
- No—must review standards of conduct each year at performance appraisal time.
- Married to an attorney.
- As a part of master's degree program 22 years ago.
- American Board of Criminalistics (ABC) certification.
- Yes, part of my Federal Bureau of Investigation (FBI) lab examiner training.
- We have guidelines to follow.

The information gathered has been very helpful in gaining a perspective to the opinions of forensic scientists. Since the initial research, positive steps have been taken regarding ethics in the profession: Ethics is now discussed more frequently; standards for training have been put in place; and laboratory accreditation requires an ethical training component. Because of the forensic scientists who recognized the need for more information sharing concerning ethics, the profession as a whole is more willing to discuss, question, and regulate ethical behavior of its members. Forensic science is a field in which ethics is of utmost importance; the profession has taken a proactive approach to increasing the ethical standard of its members.

Appendix B: Additional U.S. Forensic Science Professional Codes of Ethics

The California Association of Criminalistics (CAC)

This Code is intended as a guide to the ethical conduct of individual workers in the field of criminalistics. It is not to be construed that these principles are immutable laws nor that they are all-inclusive. Instead, they represent general standards which each worker should strive to meet. It is to be realized that each individual case may vary, just as does the evidence with which the criminalist is concerned, and no set of guides or rules will precisely fit every occasion. At the same time the fundamentals set forth in this code are to be regarded as indicating, to a considerable extent, the conduct requirements expected of members of the profession and of this association. The failure to meet or maintain certain of these standards will justifiably cast doubt on an individual's fitness for this type of work. Serious or repeated infractions of these principles may be regarded as inconsistent with membership in the association.

Criminalistics is that professional occupation concerned with the scientific analysis and examination of physical evidence, its interpretation, and its presentation in court. It involves the application of principles, techniques, and methods of the physical sciences, and has as its primary objective a determination of physical facts that may be significant in legal cases.

It is the duty of any person practicing the profession of criminalistics to serve the interests of justice to the best of his ability at all times. In fulfilling this duty, he will use all of the scientific means at his command to ascertain all of the significant physical facts relative to the matters under investigation. Having made factual determinations, the criminalist must then interpret and evaluate his findings. In this he will be guided by experience and knowledge that, coupled with a serious consideration of his analytical findings and the application of sound judgment, may enable him to arrive at opinions and conclusions pertaining to the matters under study. These findings of fact and his conclusions and opinions should then be reported, with all the accuracy and skill of which the criminalist is capable, to the end that all may fully understand and be able to place the findings in their proper relationship to the problem at issue.

In carrying out these functions, the criminalist will be guided by the those practices and procedures that are generally recognized within the profession to be consistent with a high level of professional ethics. The motives, methods, and actions of the criminalist shall at all times be above reproach, in good taste, and consistent with proper moral conduct.

I. Ethics Relating to Scientific Method

A. The criminalist has a truly scientific spirit and should be inquiring, progressive, logical, and unbiased.

B. The true scientist will make adequate examination of his materials, applying those tests essential to proof. He will not, merely for the sake of bolstering his conclusions, use unwarranted and superfluous tests in an attempt to give apparent greater weight to his results.

C. The modern scientific mind is an open one incompatible with secrecy of method. Scientific analyses will not be conducted by "secret processes," nor will conclusions in case work be based upon such tests and experiments as will not be revealed to the profession.

D. A proper scientific method demands reliability of validity in the materials analyzed. Conclusions will not be drawn from materials which themselves appear unrepresentative, atypical, or unreliable.

E. A truly scientific method requires that no generally discredited or unreliable procedure be utilized in the analysis.

F. The progressive worker will keep abreast of new developments in scientific methods and in all cases view them with an open mind. This is not to say that he need not be critical of untried or unproved methods, but he will recognize superior methods, if and when they are introduced.

II. Ethics Relating to Opinions and Conclusions

A. Valid conclusions call for the application of proven methods. Where it is practical to do so, the competent criminalist will apply such methods throughout. This does not demand the application of "standard test procedures", but, where practical, use should be made of those methods developed and recognized by this or other professional societies.

B. Tests are designed to disclose true facts and all interpretations shall be consistent with that purpose and will not be knowingly distorted.

C. Where appropriate to the correct interpretation of a test, experimental controls shall be made for verification.

D. Where possible, the conclusions reached as a result of analytical tests are properly verified by re-testing or the application of additional techniques.

E. Where test results are inconclusive or indefinite, any conclusions drawn shall be fully explained.

F. The scientific mind is unbiased and refuses to be swayed by evidence or matters outside the specific materials under consideration. It is immune to suggestion, pressures and coercions inconsistent with the evidence at hand, being interested only in ascertaining facts.

G. The criminalist will be alert to recognize the significance of a test result as it may relate to the investigative aspects of a case. In this respect he will, however, scrupulously avoid confusing scientific fact with investigative theory in his interpretations.

H. Scientific method demands that the individual be aware of his own limitations and refuse to extend himself beyond them. It is both proper and advisable that the scientific worker seek knowledge in new fields; he will not, however, be hasty to apply such knowledge before he has had adequate training and experience.

I. Where test results are capable of being interpreted to the advantage of either side of a case, the criminalist will not choose that interpretation favoring the side by which he is employed merely as a means to justify his employment.

J. It is both wise and proper that the criminalist be aware of the various possible implications of his opinions and conclusions and be prepared to weigh them, if called upon to do so. In any such case, however, he will clearly distinguish between that which may be regarded as scientifically demonstrated fact and that which is speculative.

III. Ethical Aspects of Court Presentation

A. The expert witness is one who has substantially greater knowledge of a given subject or science than has the average person. An expert opinion is properly defined as "the formal opinion of an expert." Ordinary opinion consists of one's thoughts or beliefs on matters, generally unsupported by detailed analysis of the subject under consideration. Expert opinion is also defined as the considered opinion of an expert, or a formal Judgment. It is to be understood that an "expert opinion" is an opinion derived only from a formal consideration of a subject within the expert's knowledge and experience.

B. The ethical expert does not take advantage of his privilege to express opinions by offering opinions on matters within his field of qualification which he has not given formal consideration.

C. Regardless of legal definitions, the criminalist will realize that there are degrees of certainty represented under the single term of "expert opinion." He will not take advantage of the general privilege to assign greater significance to an interpretation than is justified by the available data.

D. Where circumstances indicate it to be proper, the expert will not hesitate to indicate that while he has an opinion, derived of study, and judgment within his field, the opinion may lack the certainty of other opinions he might offer. By this or other means, he takes care to leave no false impressions in the minds of the jurors or the court.

E. In all respects, the criminalist will avoid the use of terms and opinions which will be assigned greater weight than are due them. Where an opinion requires qualification or explanation, it is not only proper but incumbent upon the witness to offer such qualification.

F. The expert witness should keep in mind that the lay juror is apt to assign greater or less significance to ordinary words of a scientist than to the same words when used by a lay witness. The criminalist, therefore, will avoid such terms as may be misconstrued or misunderstood.

G. It is not the object of the criminalist's appearance in court to present only that evidence which supports the view of the side which employs him. He has a moral obligation to see to it that the court understands the evidence as it exists and to present it in an impartial manner.

H. The criminalist will not by implication, knowingly or intentionally, assist the contestants in a case through such tactics as will implant a false impression in the minds of the jury.

I. The criminalist, testifying as an expert witness, will make every effort to use understandable language in his explanations and demonstrations in order that the jury will obtain a true and valid concept of the testimony. The use of unclear, misleading, circuitous, or ambiguous language with a view of confusing an issue in the minds of the court or jury is unethical.

J. The criminalist will answer all questions put to him in a clear, straight-forward manner and refuse to extend himself beyond his field of competence.

K. Where the expert must prepare photographs or offer oral "background information" to the jury in respect to a specific type of analytic method, this information shall be reliable and valid, typifying the usual or normal basis for the method. The instructional material shall be of that level which will provide the jury with a proper basis for evaluating the subsequent evidence presentations, and not such as would provide them with a lower standard than the science demands.

L. Any and all photographic displays shall be made according to accept-able practice, and shall not be intentionally altered or distorted with a view to misleading court or jury.

M. By way of conveying information to the court, it is appropriate that any of a variety of demonstrative materials and methods be uti-lized by the expert witness. Such methods and materials shall not, however, be unduly sensational.

IV. Ethics Relating to the General Practice of Criminalistics

A. Where the criminalist engages in private practice, it is appropriate that he set a reasonable fee for his services.

B. No services shall ever be rendered on a contingency fee basis.

C. It shall be regarded as ethical for one criminalist to re-examine evi-dence materials previously submitted to or examined by another. Where a difference of opinion arises, however, as to the significance of the evidence or to test results, it is in the interest of the profession that every effort be made by both analysts to resolve their conflict before the case goes to trial.

D. Generally, the principle of "attorney-client" relationship is consid-ered to apply to the work of a physical evidence consultant, except in a situation where a miscarriage of justice might occur. Justice should be the guiding principle.

E. It shall be ethical for one of this profession to serve an attorney in an advisory capacity regarding the interrogation of another expert who may be presenting testimony. This service must be performed in good faith and not maliciously. Its purpose is to prevent incompetent testimony but not to thwart justice.

V. Ethical Responsibilities to the Profession

In order to advance the profession of criminalistics, to promote the purposes for which the Association was formed, and encourage harmonious relation-ships between all criminalists of the State, each criminalist has an obliga-tion to conduct himself according to certain principles. These principles are no less matters of ethics than those outlined above. They differ primarily in being for the benefit of the profession rather than specific obligations to soci-ety. They, therefore, concern individuals and departments in their relation-ship with one another, business policies, and similar matters.

A. It is in the interest of the profession that information concerning any new discoveries, developments or techniques applicable to the field of criminalistics be made available to criminalists generally. A reasonable attempt should be made by any criminalist having knowledge of such developments to publicize or otherwise inform the profession of them.

B. Consistent with this and like objectives, it is expected that the attention of the profession will be directed toward any tests or methods in use which appear invalid or unreliable in order that they may be properly investigated.

C. In the interest of the profession, the individual criminalist should refrain from seeking publicity for himself or his accomplishments on specific cases. The preparation of papers for publication in appropriate media, however, is considered proper.

D. The criminalist shall discourage the association of his name with developments, publications, or organizations in which he has played no significant part, merely as a means of gaining personal publicity or prestige.

E. The C.A.C. has been organized primarily to encourage a free exchange of ideas and information between members. It is, therefore, incumbent upon each member to treat with due respect those statements and offerings made by his associates. It is appropriate that no member shall unnecessarily repeat statements or beliefs of another as expressed at C.A.C. seminars.

F. It shall be ethical and proper for one criminalist to bring to the attention of the Association a violation of any of these ethical principles. Indeed, it shall be mandatory where it appears that a serious infraction or repeated violations have been committed and where other appropriate corrective measures (if pursued) have failed.

G. This Code may be used by any criminalist in justification of his conduct in a given case with the understanding that he will have the full support of this Association.

Midwestern Association of Forensic Scientists (MAFs)

This code is intended to provide guidelines for members of the Midwestern Association of Forensic Scientists, Inc. in the performance of their professional duties. It is realized that not every situation can be covered, and this Code is neither intended to be all inconclusive nor to be a strict set of rules. It is designed to provide a basis for proper and ethical conduct in performing scientific examination and analysis, the reporting of the results to involved parties and providing testimony as an expert witness in a court of law.

For the purposes of describing the areas covered by this Code, Forensic Science is considered to include the examination and/or analysis of physical evidence regardless of its source or type; the results of which are reported for the purpose of adding information to the Criminal Justice Process. In all professional actions, it is the responsibility of each member to conduct himself in a manner that is above reproach even if a particular situation is not covered by this Code. In addition, each member's personal conduct should be on such a level that it does not cast doubt upon his reliability or integrity.

The scientific process, in relation to physical evidence, is in most instances a three-step process. First, conducting various analyses and examinations; second, formation and reporting of results and conclusions; and third, providing opinions as an expert in a court of law. It is expected that each member of the Association will conduct each step to the best of his abilities and within the framework of the Code. Serious or repeated violations of this Code may be regarded as inconsistent with acceptance into, or continuation of, membership in the Association.

I. Ethics Relating to Examination and Analyses

A. All inquires are to be approached with an open mind, with minimum anticipation as to what the results might be.

B. Any procedure used is to be open for scrutiny by members of the profession. If there is any doubt in an individual's mind as to the validity of a procedure, it is his responsibility to bring this before other members of the profession for review.

C. Proper scientific method requires reliable materials. Standards or reagents of questionable quality are to be avoided.

D. Tests may be conducted on evidential materials that may be inadequate in some way, but, these inadequacies must be kept in mind when forming conclusions.

E. Examinations and analyses are to be as complete as possible, but, additional tests which add nothing of significance are not to be utilized for the purpose of giving an opinion more weight.

F. All individuals should keep abreast of new techniques, but unproven techniques should not be used without thorough investigation and the support of proven ones. Methods that have been proved inaccurate or unreliable should not be used.

G. Wherever appropriate, controls and standards are to be utilized to conduct examinations and analyses.

H. Examinations and/or analyses that are beyond the state of an individual's experience should be reviewed by another who has adequate knowledge in the area.

II. Ethics Relating to Opinions and Conclusions

A. Conclusions formed and opinions rendered are to be based on generally accepted tests and procedures. New and/or experimental techniques may be used to add information, but, they are not to be used as the primary basis for a conclusion until proven scientifically sound.

B. Opinions are to be stated so as to be clear in their meaning. Working should not be such that inferences are drawn which are not valid, or that slant the opinion in a particular direction.

C Conclusions should be based on the information drawn from the evidence itself, not on extraneous information from other sources. Opinions stated in a scientific report should have a similar basis.

D. Sound scientific procedure requires that an individual neither form conclusions nor render opinions which are beyond his area of expertise. This is not intended to discourage exploration into new areas, but statement of opinions are to be based on adequate knowledge.

III. Ethics Relating to Testimony

A. An expert witness is defined as one who has substantially greater knowledge and experience in a particular field than the average individual. As such, he is qualified to state opinions pertaining to that field in a court of law. In addition, expert opinions stated on matters relating to Forensic Science are generally based on factual information obtained by a scientific process.

B. Considering the above, the individual testifying should make it clear in his testimony which opinions he is providing are in specific tests conducted and which are based primarily on his knowledge and experience. Likewise, if any opinions are based on information in the case other than or in addition to the scientific tests conducted, this should be clearly stated.

C. No statement should be made which might create an impression, or cause the lay person to draw a conclusion that is not warranted by the results of tests conducted.

D. If a question is put to the expert with the requirement that they should give a simple answer (i.e., yes or no), but it requires qualifications to avoid misleading the judge or jury, the expert should so state before answering the question.

E. All explanations and testimony should utilize terminology such that it is easily understood by the court and/or jury.

F. All questions asked should be answered in a clear, straightforward manner, but the witness should refuse to extend himself beyond his area of expertise.

G. All exhibits used to demonstrate the results obtained from examinations and analyses are to be prepared according to accepted procedures. They are to be presented so as to be informative, but not misleading.

IV. Ethics Relating to General Matters

A. It is appropriate that a reasonable fee be charged for private examination and analysis. This is to be based on the amount of work done, not the results obtained or a contingency basis.

B. It shall be regarded as ethical to re-examine work done by another. However, it is considered proper to insist on information as to the type of previous work so as to determine if significant changes in condition of the material might have occurred. If there is a conflict of results, every effort should be made to resolve this prior to trial.

C. Providing information for proper questioning of an expert to bring to light incompetent testimony is considered ethical. The purpose shall not be to harass the witness or to thwart justice.

V. Responsibilities toward Improvement of the Profession

Proper conduct involves more than merely refraining from a list of "don'ts" or strictly adhering to a narrow list of "do's." Members and prospective members of the Association are encouraged to work toward their own professional improvement and also the field of Forensic Sciences.

A. Each person not only has a responsibility to keep himself up to date, but also bring to the attention of others new ideas, problems encountered and other pertinent information. This includes apparent flaws in existing or new procedures.

B. Professional reporting of significant events is proper, but this should not be for the promotion of personal publicity. This particularly applies to accomplishments in specific cases.

C. It shall be ethical for a member to bring to the attention of the Association the unethical action of another. In fact, it shall be considered a breach of ethics to knowingly conceal consistent unethical action.

Southwestern Association of Forensic Sciences (SWAFs) Code of Professional Conduct

This code is intended to be a guideline for members of and those seeking membership in the Southwestern Association of Forensic Scientists (SWAFS) to provide a basis for their proper and ethical conduct. It is recognized that no set of guidelines can deal with every circumstance and this code is neither intended to be all-inclusive nor a strict set of rules.

Every member of and those seeking membership in SWAFS shall refrain from exercising professional or personal conduct adverse to the best interests and purpose of the Association. Constitution and By-Laws as amended October 11, 2007, at Fall Meeting in Austin, Texas Page 15.

Any member who violates any of the provisions of this Code of Conduct (Article Thirteen) shall be liable to probation, censure, suspension, or expulsion by action of the Board of Directors as provided in Section 6 below. Any person seeking membership shall be denied membership if any violation(s) of the provisions of this code of conduct are discovered or disclosed to the Board of Directors, membership committee, or professional conduct committee.

> "Criminalistics is an occupation that has all the responsibility of medicine, the intricacy of the law, and the universality of science. Inasmuch as it carries higher penalties for error than other professions, it is not a matter to take lightly, nor to trust to luck..."

Paul L. Kirk, Ph.D., 1902–1970

The word *forensic* is defined in the *Academic Press* Dictionary of Science and Technology as "of or relating to courts of law or legal proceedings..."

Existence of the forensic science profession is undeniably linked to the justice system. Jury decisions are based in part on the opinions presented to them by forensic "experts." Trial verdicts are reached from these jury decisions. Forensic scientists therefore have an obligation to provide opinions and facts to a court of law that are truthful, honorable, and of sound judgment. Conclusions and opinions must not be compromised, misrepresented, embellished nor exaggerated. Testimonial negligence will result in the utmost crime against humanity. No person shall... "be deprived of life, liberty or property without due process of law" (Fifth Amendment as referenced by Kusmack).

Preparation for civil and/or criminal law matters must be given great attention and should commence early on during one's career. Previous sections have discussed ideals that empower forensic scientists in their abilities to successfully execute the duties of their job. The work product of the forensic scientist is culminated in the conclusions stated in their report and during testimony.

"Always tell the truth; that way you never have to remember what you said."

Harry S. Truman

Communication pertaining to forensic legal matters, nevertheless, must be succinct yet thorough and understandable. Ron Smith states "It is certainly possible for you to tell the complete truth about your knowledge of the case but to have done it in such a fashion as to make it unbelievable to anyone that hears it."

The obligations of forensic testimony are almost infinite. The SWAFS Code will not ensure that its members are respectful, honest, fair, and responsible, but it will ensure that persons not upholding their responsibility to the profession are aware of the consequences of their negligent actions.

Nicholas T. Kuzmach, J.D., M.A., "Legal Aspects of Forensic Science" In Forensic Science Handbook. Richard Saferstein, Editor. 1982. Chapter 1. Constitution and By-Laws as amended October 11, 2007, at Fall Meeting in Austin, Texas Page 16.
Ron Smith "Courtroom Testimony Techniques: Success instead of Survival" Meridian Mississippi.

I. Ethics Relating to General Criminalistic Matters

Each SWAFS member is to give the best possible services in all cases, irrespective of the importance of the matter and in any case in which surrounding circumstances seriously restrict an adequate examination should be appropriately recorded.

A. It is considered proper for a forensic scientist to evaluate evidence previously examined by another. Any discrepancies noted should be discussed prior to the case going to court. The ultimate goal should be an objective assessment of the evidence.
B. A reasonable fee may be charged for private examination and analyses. This is to be based on the amount of work performed, not the results obtained or on a contingency fee basis.
C. It shall be the responsibility of every SWAFS member to uphold the laws unto which they are bound, at both the federal and state levels.
D. A good faith effort shall be made by both SWAFS and SWAFS members to promote and receive quality training.

II. Ethical Responsibilities to the Profession

A. Each SWAFS member must be law abiding and avoid behavior leading to the arrest and conviction of a felony or crimes involving moral turpitude.

B. A member convicted of a felony may have membership in SWAFS revoked.

C. Conviction of DWI, possession/use of drugs or possession of marijuana may be cause for revocation of SWAFS membership.

D. It shall be a violation of this code for a member of SWAFS to willingly tolerate unethical activity on the part of another member.

E. Members have a responsibility to keep abreast of advances in the forensic field and the open sharing of information concerning new techniques and developments in the field.

F. The forensic scientist may only release information or classified law enforcement information to authorized personnel as commanded by their state law, agency policy, and agency practices.

III. Ethics Relating to Examination and Analyses

A. Evidentiary examinations should be undertaken with an objective frame of mind.

B. The forensic scientist will make a thorough examination of evidence, applying a sufficient number of tests to reach a conclusion.

C. Only methodology currently accepted in the field shall be used. New techniques shall be thoroughly validated before use. Constitution and By-Laws as amended October 11, 2007, at Fall Meeting in Austin, Texas Page 17.

IV. Ethics Relating to Opinions and Conclusions

A. Statements pertaining to the results and conclusions of an examination must be objective in nature, keeping in mind the current capabilities of forensic science.

B. Opinions based on study, experience, and judgment should be distinguished from those based on facts derived from scientific evaluation.

C. Conclusions must be based on the information gained from the evidence, not on extraneous information from other sources. Opinions stated in a scientific report must have a similar basis.

D. Opinions must be stated as clearly and succinctly as is practical, both on reports and in legal proceedings, to prevent miscommunication. Extraneous and superfluous verbiage should be avoided.

E. The analyst must not render opinions, which are beyond his/her area of expertise or beyond the current capabilities of the analysis performed.

V. Ethics Relating to Testimony/Courtroom Presentation

A. A member of SWAFS must refrain from misrepresentation of education, experience, or area of expertise. It is imperative that the forensic scientist be aware of personal limitations in training and experience.
B. No statement shall be made to intentionally create an impression or cause the layperson to draw a conclusion that is not warranted by the results of the tests conducted.
C. All explanations and testimony should utilize terminology such that is easily understood by the court and/or jury.

VI. Rules and Procedures

In order to be aware of the ethical standards expected by SWAFS and possible violations of the Code of Conduct, every member will receive a copy of the Code whether it is incorporated into the By-Laws or becomes a separate publication of its own. It is the responsibility of the individual member to read the Code and be aware of its implications.

Unethical conduct detrimental to the profession or serious unethical conduct per se, which is not specified herein are also considered violations of the Code.

If a member against whom a grievance has been filed terminates his/her membership, a record will be maintained in the member's file that the termination of membership occurred with a grievance pending.

A grievance concerning professional conduct of a member of this association must be made in writing to the Board of Directors. The Committee on Constitution and By-Laws as amended October 11, 2007, at Fall Meeting in Austin, Texas Page 18.

A. Professional Conduct shall investigate any ethical matters submitted in writing to the Board of Directors. The Committee shall present a written report to the Board of Directors upon completion of the investigation.
B. The Board of Directors shall review the report and determine if any action shall be taken against the member cited. The Board of Directors, by a majority vote, can determine the course of action to be taken: expulsion, suspension, censure, or probation.

a. Expulsion: The member will be notified of expulsion and given the right to meet with the board to deny, defend, refute, any actions in question. This can occur via phone conference, at the annual meeting, or other means acceptable by the BOD. A final decision will be voted on by the Board and a majority vote will prevail. Any subsequent information that is provided to the BOD or Committee will be used in considering reactivation of membership but is at the discretion of the BOD.

b. Suspension: The member will be notified of suspension and given the right to meet with the board to deny, defend, refute, any actions in question. This can occur via phone conference, at the annual meeting, or other means acceptable by the BOD. A final decision and length of suspension will be voted on by the Board and a majority vote will prevail. Any subsequent information that is provided to the BOD or Committee will be used in considering lifting the suspension. The BOD may also recommend a course of action that the suspended member must undergo in order to have the suspension lifted.

c. Censure: The member will be notified of censure and given the right to meet with the board to deny, defend, refute, any actions in question. This can occur via phone conference, at the annual meeting, or other means acceptable by the BOD. A final decision will be voted on by the Board and a majority vote will prevail. Any subsequent information that is provided to the BOD or Committee will be used in considering removing the censure. The BOD must set a time limit for the censorship and recommend a course of action that the censured member must undergo in order to have the censure removed.

d. Probation: The member will be notified of probation and given the right to meet with the board to deny, defend, refute, any actions in question. This can occur via phone conference, at the annual meeting, or other means acceptable by the BOD. A final decision will be voted on by the Board and a majority vote will prevail. Any subsequent information that is provided to the BOD or Committee will be used in considering removing the probation. The BOD may also recommend a course of action that the member must undergo in order to have the probation lifted. The probation should last no longer than one year from the time the final decision is rendered by the BOD. Constitution and By-Laws as amended October 11, 2007, at Fall Meeting in Austin, Texas Page 19.

C. The individual should be notified of the committee's and Board findings of any ethical violation, in writing, with ample time to respond, in writing, as to why a particular issue is not an ethics issue (violation of the by-laws and code of conduct). Those initial correspondences should be between the BOD and the accused based on the documented research of the committee.

D. Any member who has been suspended from membership may apply for reinstatement once the period of suspension is completed.

E. Any member expelled from this Association is no longer eligible to hold office or vote in the Association. Any dues and/or fees paid to the Association are forfeited to the association when a member is expelled.

F. If, based upon the investigation of the Committee of Professional Conduct, the Board of Directors determine that some other action is appropriate, the same protocol will be followed.

G. If, based upon the investigation of the Committee on Professional Conduct, the Board of Directors determines that no action is necessary, the matter shall be closed. The person who filed the original grievance will be notified in writing of the Board of Directors' decision.

Appendix C: U.S. Law Enforcement Professional Codes of Ethics

The International Association of Chiefs of Police (IACP)

Part I: Ethics

As set forth in Article I, Section 2 of the IACP Constitution, the International Association of Chiefs of Police is firmly committed to the principle that law enforcement officers must achieve and maintain the highest standard of ethics.

If a member of the association fails to uphold this standard of ethics or otherwise conducts themselves in such a manner to bring the Association into disrepute, the Executive Committee may act under the authority provided in Article 1, Section 12 of the IACP Constitution to discipline, suspend or expel such member.

Part II: Conflicts of Interest

Section 1: Purpose

The Association has determined that its effective governance depends in large measure on deliberate, thoughtful, and disinterested decision making by the IACP leadership and staff.

Because the Association's reputation and ability to carry out its mission can be seriously damaged by the appearance or suggestion of a conflict of interest, the Executive Committee has created this Conflict of Interest Rule.

Section 2: Application

The policies and requirements identified in this Rule apply to certain individuals associated with IACP that make and implement Association policy. These include members of the Executive Committee, Board of Officers, the Parliamentarian, Chairs of IACP Committees and Sections, the Executive Director, the Chief of Staff and all staff division directors.

Section 3: Policy

None of the individuals identified in Section 2 of this Rule shall use their position, or the knowledge gained there from, in such a manner that a conflict between the interest of the Association and their personal interests or business arises. Personal interests or business in this policy are limited to pecuniary, financial, issues. Conflicts would surface in those situations in which an individual would use their organizational position to advance a personal agenda at the organization's expense.

Each of these individuals has a duty of loyalty to place the interest of the Association foremost in any dealing with the Association and has a continuing responsibility to comply with the requirements of this policy. This loyalty specifically requires that these individuals refrain from knowingly engaging in any activity that would place them, or any other organizations with whom they are associated, in a competitive posture with the Association on any matter.

The conduct of personal business between any of these individuals and this Association must be disclosed and is prohibited. If any of these individuals has an interest in a proposed transaction with the Association or any of its Divisions, Sections, or Committees in the form of any significant personal financial interest in the transaction or in any organization involved in the transaction, or holds a position of influence in any such organization, they must make full disclosure of such interest before any discussion or negotiation of such transaction.

Individuals identified in Section 2 who are aware of a potential conflict of interest with respect to any matter coming before the Association shall not be present for any discussion of or vote in connection with the matter.

Section 4: Disclosure

Implementation of the policy stated in Section 3 requires that the individuals addressed by this Rule will submit annual reports on the form specified in Section 5, below. In addition, these individuals will, if not previously disclosed, make disclosure before any relevant action.

Reports submitted, when there is a need, will be filed with the Executive Director and reviewed by an Ethics Committee which will attempt to resolve any actual or potential conflict(s). Any conflict issue that cannot be resolved by the Ethics Committee will be referred to the Executive Committee for final resolution.

Section 5: Disclosure Form

Individuals addressed by this Rule will, by November 15 of each year, be required to submit the following conflict of interest form to the Executive Director: R16 IACP CONSTITUTION (REV. 10/30/06).

Conflict-Of-Interest Questionnaire

Please answer all questions. If the answer is yes, please explain. An affirmative response does not necessarily imply that the relationship is improper or that it should be terminated.

1. Have you or any related party had any material interest, direct or indirect, in any transaction since you started working with the IACP to which the Association or any of its Divisions, Sections, or Committees was or is to be a party?
   – Yes   – No

2. If your answer is yes, please describe the relationship including any financial dealings.

3. Do you or any related party have any material interest, direct or indirect, in any pending or incomplete transaction to which the Association or any of its Divisions, Sections, or Committees was or is to be a party?
   – Yes   – No

4. If your answer is yes, please describe the relationship including any financial dealings.

5. Since you started working with the IACP, have you or any related party1 been indebted to the Association or any of its Divisions, Sections, or Committees? Please exclude amounts due for ordinary travel and expense advances and for outstanding pledges.
   – Yes   – No

6. If your answer is yes, please indicate the type of indebtedness and the amount.

7. Please provide a complete list of all organizations like the IACP, apart from your primary place of employment, with whom you currently work and from whom you receive compensation for services provided.

8. Please provide a complete list of any law enforcement-related organizations in which you are a member. Also, please indicate if you serve in any influential capacity that is apart from your status as a member.

9. The answers to the foregoing questions are accurately stated to the best of my knowledge and belief.

Signature: _____ Date: _____

1. Related party is defined as members of your immediate family, which includes your spouse, minor children, and all other dependents; estates, trusts, and partnerships in which you or your immediate family has a present or vested future beneficial interest; and a corporation in which you or your immediate family is a beneficial owner of more than 5 percent of the voting interests.
2. Answers to these questions should be as complete as possible. Individuals are encouraged to err on the side of providing more information than necessary where they are uncertain about how to respond to questions posed.

American Correctional Association (ACA)

The American Correctional Association expects of its members unfailing honesty, respect for the dignity and individuality of human beings and a commitment to professional and compassionate service. To this end, we subscribe to the following principles.

1. Members shall respect and protect the civil and legal rights of all individuals.
2. Members shall treat every professional situation with concern for the welfare of the individuals involved and with no intent to personal gain.
3. Members shall maintain relationships with colleagues to promote mutual respect within the profession and improve the quality of service.
4. Members shall make public criticism of their colleagues or their agencies only when warranted, verifiable, and constructive.
5. Members shall respect the importance of all disciplines within the criminal justice system and work to improve cooperation with each segment.
6. Members shall honor the public's right to information and share information with the public to the extent permitted by law subject to individuals' right to privacy.
7. Members shall respect and protect the right of the public to be safeguarded from criminal activity.
8. Members shall refrain from using their positions to secure personal privileges or advantages.

9. Members shall refrain from allowing personal interest to impair objectivity in the performance of duty while acting in an official capacity.

10. Members shall refrain from entering into any formal or informal activity or agreement which presents a conflict of interest or is inconsistent with the conscientious performance of duties.

11. Members shall refrain from accepting any gifts, services, or favors that is or appears to be improper or implies an obligation inconsistent with the free and objective exercise of professional duties.

12. Members shall clearly differentiate between personal views/statements and views/statements/positions made on behalf of the agency or Association.

13. Members shall report to appropriate authorities any corrupt or unethical behaviors in which there is sufficient evidence to justify review.

14. Members shall refrain from discriminating against any individual because of race, gender, creed, national origin, religious affiliation, age, disability, or any other type of prohibited discrimination.

15. Members shall preserve the integrity of private information; they shall refrain from seeking information on individuals beyond that which is necessary to implement responsibilities and perform their duties; members shall refrain from revealing nonpublic information unless expressly authorized to do so.

16. Members shall make all appointments, promotions, and dismissals in accordance with established civil service rules, applicable contract agreements, and individual merit, rather than furtherance of personal interests.

17. Members shall respect, promote, and contribute to a work place that is safe, healthy, and free of harassment in any form.

American Jail Association

As an officer employed in a detention/correctional capacity, I swear (or affirm) to be a good citizen and a credit to my community, state, and nation at all times. I will abstain from questionable behavior which might bring disrepute to the agency for which I work, my family, my community, and my associates. My lifestyle will be above and beyond reproach and I will constantly strive to set an example of a professional who performs his/her duties according to the laws of our country, state, and community and the policies, procedures, written and verbal orders, and regulations of the agency for which I work.

On the job I promise to:

KEEP	The institution secure so as to safeguard my community and the lives of the staff, inmates, and visitors on the premises.
WORK	With each individual firmly and fairly without regard to rank, status, or condition.
MAINTAIN	A positive demeanor when confronted with stressful situations of scorn, ridicule, danger, and/or chaos.
REPORT	Either in writing or by word of mouth to the proper authorities those things which should be reported, and keep silent about matters which are to remain confidential according to the laws and rules of the agency and government.
MANAGE	And supervise the inmates in an evenhanded and courteous manner.
REFRAIN	At all times from becoming personally involved in the lives of the inmates and their families.
TREAT	All visitors to the jail with politeness and respect and do my utmost to ensure that they observe the jail regulations.
TAKE	Advantage of all education and training opportunities designed to assist me to become a more competent officer.
COMMUNICATE	With people in or outside of the jail, whether by phone, written word, or word of mouth, in such a way so as not to reflect in a negative manner upon my agency.
CONTRIBUTE	To a jail environment which will keep the inmate involved in activities designed to improve his/her attitude and character.
SUPPORT	All activities of a professional nature through membership and participation that will continue to elevate the status of those who operate our nation's jails. Do my best through word and deed to present an image to the public at large of a jail professional, committed to progress for an improved and enlightened criminal justice system.

The American Jail Association's Board of Directors has approved the AJA Code of Ethics as part of an integral program to achieve a high standard of professional conduct among those officers employed in our nation's jails. Adopted by the American Jail Association Board of Directors on November 10, 1991. Revised May 19, 1993.

National Sheriffs' Association

Code of Ethics of the Office of Sheriff

As a constitutionally/statutorily elected sheriff, I recognize and accept that I am given a special trust and confidence by the citizens and employees whom I have been elected to serve, represent, and manage. This trust and confidence is my bond to ensure that I shall behave and act according to the highest personal and professional standards. In furtherance of this pledge, I will abide by the following Code of Ethics.

I shall ensure that I and my employees, in the performance of our duties, will enforce and administer the law according to the standards of the U.S. Constitution and applicable state constitutions and statutes so that equal protection of the law is guaranteed to everyone. To that end I shall not permit personal opinion, party affiliations, or consideration of the status of others to alter or lessen this standard of treatment of others.

I shall establish, promulgate, and enforce a set of standards of behavior of my employees which will govern the overall management and operation of the law enforcement functions, court related activities, and corrections operations of my agency.

I shall not tolerate nor condone brutal or inhumane treatment of others by my employees nor shall I permit or condone inhumane or brutal treatment of inmates in my care and custody.

I strictly adhere to standards of fairness and integrity in the conduct of campaigns for election and I shall conform to all applicable statutory standards of election financing and reporting so that the Office of Sheriff is not harmed by the actions of myself or others.

I shall routinely conduct or have conducted an internal and external audit of the public funds entrusted to my care and publish this information so that citizens can be informed about my stewardship of these funds.

I shall follow the accepted principles of efficient and effective administration and management as the principal criteria for my judgments and decisions in the allocation of resources and services in law enforcement, court related, and corrections functions of my office.

I shall hire and promote only those employees or others who are the very best candidates for a position according to accepted standards of objectivity and merit. I shall not permit other factors to influence hiring or promotion practice.

I shall ensure that all employees are granted and receive relevant training supervision in the performance of their duties so that competent and excellent service is provided by the Office of Sheriff.

I shall ensure that during my tenure as sheriff, I shall not use the Office of Sheriff for private gain.

I accept and adhere to this code of ethics. In so doing, I also accept responsibility for encouraging others in my profession to abide by this Code.

Appendix D:
International Forensic
Science Professional
Codes of Ethics

Australian Federal Police

Professional Standards

The Australian Federal Police (AFP) operates in an increasingly complex and dynamic environment. It is critical to the continued success of the AFP that the organisation maintains the confidence and trust of the Australian government, national and international partners and the Australian community which it serves.

Central to the confidence and trust placed in the AFP is the integrity and professionalism of AFP appointees and the ability of the organisation to prevent and counter fraud and corruption.

The term 'Professional Standards' relates to the expectations the Commissioner has of all AFP appointees and the functional area of the AFP that deals with professional standards issues.

These 'Professional Standards' of AFP appointees are underpinned by the AFP Core Values and the AFP Code of Conduct.

AFP Professional Standards is responsible for developing and maintaining the highest professional standards throughout the organisation including the oversight and investigation of complaints about the conduct of AFP appointees.

Minor complaints will be actioned by managers within the workplace and oversighted by Professional Standards.

Serious complaints will be investigated by the Professional Standards.

Complaints relating to corruption matters will be referred by the AFP Commissioner to the Australian Commission for Law Enforcement Integrity (ACLEI) for appropriate action.

All complaints are subject to external oversight by the Commonwealth Law Enforcement Ombudsman and corruption matters are subject to oversight by the ACLEI.

AFP Core Values

Fundamental to compliance with the professional standards of the AFP is a requirement to adhere to the core values of the organisation. The core values of the AFP are as follows:

Integrity

Integrity is a core requirement of the AFP. On an individual level, integrity is displayed through soundness of moral principle, honesty and sincerity.

As an organisation, the AFP demonstrates integrity through:

- A genuine commitment to the success of individuals.
- Complete honesty and forthrightness in all commitments with people.
- High standards of personal conduct and character at all times.
- Complete trustworthiness when handling property, money and information.

Commitment

Commitment is characterised by dedication, application, perseverance and a belief in your ability to achieve and add value.

In the AFP, commitment is displayed when individuals:

- Apply themselves to all tasks/jobs for which they have responsibility.
- Persist with jobs until objectives are achieved or are no longer reasonably attainable.
- Strive to uphold the vision and mission of the AFP.
- Strive to achieve individual, team and corporate milestones.

Excellence

The AFP believes there is always room for improvement – and that the never-ending search for improvement leads to excellence. We aim for excellence in everything we do.

To promote excellence at the AFP we:

- Empower our employees and involve them in providing a quality service.
- Coach and develop people rather than control and direct them.

- Strive to deliver the product that best serves the needs of our clients.
- Constantly improve work performance by seeking to remove waste and inefficiencies.
- Dedicate time and effort to self improvement.
- Encourage innovation, experimentation and risk taking.
- Support teamwork by: communicating with each other; participating together with problem solving; sharing work; delegating and taking responsibility for individual tasks; dealing with conflict, performance problems and discipline issues.

Accountability

Accountability is about ownership of work or results, and being answerable for outcomes.

In the AFP, this means we:

- Accept personal responsibility for the consequences of our efforts.
- Ensure people know what is expected of them, how their work will be evaluated and how success is measured or determined.
- Allow individuals and teams to make decisions about their work.
- Do not assume credit for the work of others.
- Give feedback on work performance.

Fairness

Fairness means being impartial and equitable.

In the AFP, that means we:

- Respect people as individuals and for their differences.
- Apply anti-discrimination, fairness and equity principles in our daily work.
- Do not act from malice, prejudice or personal bias when making decisions.
- Approach people and issues with tolerance and an open mind.

Trust

Trust means having faith and confidence, and being able to rely and depend on others.

In the AFP, that means we:

- Assume people can be relied on to do the right thing.
- Declare conflicts of interest if they arise.
- Do not subject people to abuses of power.
- Respect each other regardless of roles and status.

- Foster an environment in which people do not fear punishment for making honest mistakes.

Canadian Society of Forensic Science

Code of Conduct

Rules of Professional Conduct

Adopted November 5, 1994

Members of the Canadian Society of Forensic Science, with respect to their responsibilities to the C.S.F.S., shall:

1. Comply with the By-laws of the Society;
2. Report to the Board, any violation of these "Rules of Professional Conduct" by another member of the Society;
3. Accept that their membership in the Society demonstrates an active interest in forensic science however, this membership does not by itself mean that they have the necessary qualifications to practice in their forensic science discipline nor does it mean that they are competent in their forensic science discipline; with respect to their responsibilities to their client, employer or to the court, shall:
4. Treat all information from an agency or client with the appropriate confidentiality;
5. Make all reasonable efforts to treat items of potential evidential value with the care and control necessary to ensure their integrity;
6. Take reasonable steps to ensure that all items in a case receive appropriate technical analysis;
7a. Utilise methods, techniques, standards and controls, provided that they exist, that they are generally accepted and that they are current and;
7b. Utilise methods and techniques with standards and controls to conduct examinations and analysis such that they could be reproduced by another qualified and competent person;
8. Make full and complete disclosure as required by law of the findings to the submitting agency or client;
9. Make and keep worknotes on all items received, the examinations done, the results obtained and the findings and conclusions made in a timely fashion;
10. Render opinions and conclusions strictly in accordance with the results and findings in the case and only to the extent justified by those results and findings;

11. Make all efforts to testify in a clear, straightforward manner and refuse to extend themselves beyond their field of expertise or level of competence;

12. Not exaggerate, embellish or otherwise misrepresent qualifications when testifying;

13. Be impartial and independent in their analysis, reporting and testimony; with respect to their responsibilities to the profession of forensic science, shall:

14. Carry out their duties in a professional manner and strive to be worthy of the confidence of the public;

15. Regard and respect their peers with the same standards that they hold for themselves;

16a. Set a reasonable fee for services if it is appropriate to do so, taking care not to set unreasonably high fees for services, not to charge fees for services not done or services that are unnecessary, while being able to reduce or waive fees;

16b. Not, under any circumstances, render services on a contingency basis; and

17. Strive to maintain and improve their skills and knowledge and to keep current with advances and standards in their discipline.

Australian and New Zealand Forensic Science Society Inc.

Code of Ethics

The code of ethics was developed to give a guide to practitioners, students and customers of forensic scientists. It sets down in plain English what is expected of a *forensic* practitioner in examining evidence, giving results and providing evidence in court.

Scientific Method

1. Accepted scientific principals and methods should be utilised unless a particular investigation requires the use of a novel method.

2. Appropriate methods should be used having regard to the standard of proof that is required and that can be reasonably achieved.

3. Objectivity should be maintained at all times, from when examining scenes and collecting items for further examination, to reaching conclusions based on available evidence.

4. Relevant experimental controls should be used and, where appropriate, results verified by retesting or by the application of additional or alternative techniques.

5. Examination should not be taken beyond the limits of one's expertise.
6. Where applicable, the physical results of tests, field notes, test notes, reports and photographs should be retained for as long as possible or at least during the currency of any relevant legal proceedings.

Reporting

1. Distinctions should be made between the results of tests and examinations, and opinions based on these. Any pertinent limitations to the test results and conclusions should be explained.
2. Opinions should be expressed in simple, precise and unambiguous terms.
3. Where test results or conclusions are capable of being interpreted to the advantage of either side in a legal proceeding, each result or conclusion should be given weight according to its merit.
4. There should be a preparedness to concede that other opinions, being contrary to or at variance with one's own can be honestly held.
5. Reference should be made in the report to all items examined or tested.
6. The nature and character of all tests and examinations should be available to the court.
7. Reports will be signed only by the persons who have either carried out the work described or have directly or indirectly supervised it.

Pre-Trial Conduct

1. Every endeavour should be made to produce the report in sufficient time before the relevant legal proceedings so as to enable proper consideration of it, provided that sufficient notification of the date of legal proceedings has been received.
2. On the understanding that there is no property in expert scientific witnesses, the prospective witness should be reasonably available for discussion with professional representatives of all parties involved with the proceedings.
3. Any retainer offered should be refused if it is suspected that a purpose of the offer is to prevent relevant evidence being presented to a Court.

Conduct in Court

1. As far as possible, simple terms should be used when giving evidence.

2. Any attempt made to press the witness to testify as to matters beyond and/or outside their expertise should be firmly resisted.

3. An objective and moderate manner in giving evidence should be cultivated.

4. In the conduct of giving evidence the witness, upon request, is under an obligation to disclose all tests and experiments performed, subject to the directions of the presiding judicial officer.

5. The witness should plainly state opinions as such and take care to distinguish them from statements of fact.

6. The witness should appeal to presiding judicial officer (in the absence of the jury if the trial be by judge and jury) if they believe that the manner in which evidence is being elicited is such to prevent the disclosure of a significant relevant matter or circumstance.

General Matters

1. It is proper to advise a lawyer concerning the reports and evidence of another expert even though such advice may be used in the cross-examination of that expert. To this end, co-operation in the provision of notes/records should be given with, if desired, the proviso of open consultation and discussion with the reviewing expert.

2. Confidential information received should not be inappropriately disclosed.

3. Media association of an expert's name with specific cases or accomplishments, or association of one's name with developments, publications or organisations with which that expert played no significant part, should be discouraged.

4. Professional and personal behaviour consistent with membership of a skilled profession should be observed and colleagues treated with due respect and inappropriate criticism of them avoided.

5. No services should be rendered where the fee is dependent on the outcome of the examination.

6. Errors or omissions discovered prior to, during or after any hearing should be disclosed.

Royal Canadian Mounted Police

Ethics and Integrity in the RCMP

The Royal Canadian Mounted Police (RCMP) is a national government organization in which all Canadians take pride. In order to keep this confidence, we have a responsibility to meet the high expectations of Canadians in both our personal and professional conduct. Our ethical behavior must be evident in everything we do.

This brochure helps set out the ethical issues surrounding the relationship between the RCMP and the private sector as well as identify legislation that must be considered when decisions are made. It covers the areas of conflict of interest, post-retirement guidelines, hospitality and acceptance of gifts, the sponsorship program and proprietary information.

The operations of the RCMP are carried out by dedicated employees in all job categories. All employees of the RCMP are responsible for ensuring we maintain a professional relationship with our business partners. While we rely on our alliances with private-sector businesses, the Canadian public expects us to ensure that public funds are spent efficiently and in the public's best interest.

RCMP ethical standards are based on six core values: integrity, honesty, professionalism, compassion, respect and accountability. These core values make up the basis of every decision we make and help us determine how we should conduct ourselves everyday. Closely following these values allows employees to make informed and ethical judgements in business dealings and the workplace. It is critical that we make sound decisions as we are accountable for them in the end.

Common sense and this guide provide a framework to help us make choices. Your own judgement and values will be at the core of your behaviour and for which you will be held accountable.

We also believe it is essential that the Canadian public and our business partners have a clear understanding of our obligations and standards. In setting out clear obligations, I believe we will maintain the trust that the Canadian public has placed in us.

Conflict of Interest

Consistent with our core values of integrity, honesty, professionalism, compassion, respect and accountability, employees are to avoid any actual, apparent or potential conflicts of interest. This applies to everyday work responsibilities and conduct. All employees must continue to uphold the organization's high standards and conduct themselves in ways that enhance the image of the RCMP. This image can be harmed by cases of outside individuals perceived to have benefitted inappropriately from their dealings with the RCMP.

Employees are to respect existing policy in relation to gifts, hospitality and benefits; declining those which are prohibited and reporting those which may be permitted. Employees are to avoid being under an obligation, or the perception of obligation, to a person or organization that might benefit from special consideration. They are to avoid preferential treatment of family, friends, and organizations in which they have an interest, in relation to official matters.

As per Section 37 of the *RCMP Act* and Part 1, Principles, of the conflict of interest and Post-Employment code for the Public Service it is essential to ensure that an employee's duties are completed without a conflict of interest, either real or perceived. All steps must be taken to ensure impartiality and fairness in relationships as well as to protect the image of the RCMP in such areas as gifts, hospitality and secondary employment.

The onus is on the employee to take whatever actions are necessary to avoid being placed in a position of conflict of interest.

Gifts

Gifts, hospitality or other benefits that could influence employees in their judgement and performance of official duties and responsibilities must be declined. Employees must not accept, directly or indirectly, any gifts, hospitality or other benefits that are offered by persons, groups or organizations having dealings with the government.

Accepting offers of incidental gifts, hospitality or other benefits arising out of activities associated with the routine performance of their official duties and responsibilities is not prohibited if such gifts, hospitality or other benefits:

- Are within the bounds of propriety, a normal expression of courtesy or within the normal standards of hospitality;
- Must not bring suspicion on the employee's objectivity and impartiality; and
- Would not compromise the integrity of the RCMP or Government of Canada.

It may be exceptionally difficult to decline gifts, hospitality or other benefits offered by individuals or organizations from different cultures with particular approaches to gifts. In such cases, every effort should be made to decline the gifts without offending the persons involved. The inherent call for personal judgement is amplified here. If it is not possible to decline the gift, hospitality or other benefits, employees must immediately report the matter to a manager or supervisor. The manager or supervisor may require that a gift of this nature be retained by the RCMP or be disposed of for charitable purposes.

All gifts, awards and bequests, if they are money or converted into money, acquired in connection with the performance of a regular or civilian member's duties are to be deposited into the Consolidated Revenue Fund to the account of the *Benefit Trust Fund* . Public Service employees are required to turn over gifts to the RCMP via their supervisor.

While the RCMP recognizes customary business practices such as offering and accepting gifts or providing and receiving hospitality benefits, it is expected that all employees of the RCMP, regardless of status, respect the law and government policies. This is especially true in the operations of the RCMP where there is a greater onus on employees to exercise discretion.

It is important to note that this guide also applies when the RCMP is the organization acting as host. It is critical that all RCMP sponsored events and their respective budgets conform to Treasury Board policy and RCMP procedures and guidelines and be approved before any funds are dispersed.

Secondary Employment—Outside Activities

Employees must seek approval from a supervisor prior to engaging in any outside activity (including secondary employment) which is likely to give rise to a real, potential or apparent conflict of interest. It is an employee's responsibility to report any outside activity that is directly or indirectly related to the employee's duties.

Members should not accept remuneration from any government department, agency, or Crown corporation without permission as per section 55 of the *RCMP Regulations*.

All employees must arrange their personal affairs in a manner that ensures they are able to meet their obligations to the RCMP, including, where applicable, emergency duties.

Post-employment Guidelines

Employees must not take improper advantage of their work experience and/or position after leaving the Force. Restrictions on post-employment may apply, especially in the time period immediately following departure from the Force. (For more information, see *Conflict of Interest and Post-Employment Code* for the Public Service)

Use of RCMP (Government of Canada) Equipment

The unauthorized personal use of RCMP equipment is prohibited. This applies to such items as computers and vehicles. Authorized personal use of vehicles is subject to current "personal use" in the *Income Tax Act* and Treasury Board Circular 1987-34: Executive Vehicles.

Use of the RCMP Name and Image

The RCMP image enjoys world-wide recognition as a primary symbol of Canada and as such it is often assumed that this image is in the public domain and can be used without restriction. This is not the case. Use of the RCMP image is in fact strictly regulated pursuant to provisions in the *Trade-marks Act*, *Copyright Act* and the *RCMP Act*.

The RCMP name and a series of RCMP images are also protected from unauthorized use by virtue of their designation as "Official mark" pursuant to paragraph 9(1)(n) of the *Trade-marks Act*. No person may use these "Official marks" without the consent of the RCMP. Contact Public Affairs and Information Directorate for more information.

RCMP Sponsorship Program

Since the genesis of the RCMP national sponsorship program in the early 1990s, the issue of ethics and conflict of interest have been at the very core of its strategic development and implementation. Beginning in 1995, the RCMP sponsorship guidelines and toolkit were developed to include sections on ethics, conflict of interest and rigorous and transparent financial accounting.

When pursuing a sponsorship agreement it is essential that all arrangements are developed on a firm foundation of ethics and a strong integrity-based approach. The policy centre for guidance on procedures and risk management assessment mechanism is Strategic Partnerships and Heritage Branch, Public Affairs and Information Directorate, at National Headquarters. Staff will be able to directly help individuals seeking advice and will guide them to toolkits developed to inform them on ways to proceed.

Protection of Information

RCMP employees will take all necessary steps to protect third party proprietary information, in compliance with the spirit and intent of the *Access to Information Act*.

There are some exemptions to the release of information. This includes, but is not limited to, security issues and proprietary information. By law, federal institutions are required to protect some proprietary information or information given in confidence by private sector suppliers of goods and services. For example trade secrets, financial, commercial, scientific and technical information confidentially supplied to a government institution can be exempted from disclosure. However, to qualify, this information must always have been treated with confidence by the third party. Information in which a disclosure could result in financial loss or prejudice the competitive position of the third party or interfere with contractual negotiations can be exempted. This is by no means an exhaustive list of exemptions but serves to act as a guide. Please refer to the *Access to Information Act* for more information

It is important to note that suppliers of goods and services to the RCMP have similar obligations. All contracts must comply with Treasury Board and

RCMP policies, standards and guidelines such as establishing safeguards for the protection of classified information provided to the supplier for the purposes of their contracts.

Senior Managers of Australian and New Zealand Forensic Science Laboratories

Code of Conduct

The Senior Managers of Australian and New Zealand Forensic Science Laboratories (SMANZFL) was formed to facilitate co-operation and support between the managers of forensic science laboratories and services in Australia and New Zealand.

Ethical conduct is a fundamental principle underpinning all professions. In order to signal management commitment to ethics it was agreed that SMANZFL would adopt the code of ethics of the Australian and New Zealand Forensic Science Society (ANZFSS).

Furthermore, SMANZFL will endeavour to provide a foundation upon which there is:

- A commitment to management practices in forensic science that ensure forensic science services have the confidence of the users and the community.
- A commitment to excellent quality management practices and the NATA and ASCLD/LAB accreditation programs.
- A commitment to training and education in the forensic sciences to ensure that the highest professional standards are achieved.
- Provide input and support to programs undertaken by the National Institute of Forensic Science (NIFS).
- Support initiatives and programs of the Australia and New Zealand Forensic Science Society (ANZFSS).
- Cooperation of managers to ensure forensic science initiatives are in the best national interest.
- Foster linkages with the wider scientific and academic communities.
- Promote SMANZFL in the international arena.
- An exchange of information and professional support mechanisms to those within the forensic science disciplines in Australia and New Zealand.
- A working environment that actively encourages employees to pursue the highest attainable competencies and ethical work practices.
- The positive promotion of the forensic sciences as an important component of the Criminal Justice Systems in Australia and New Zealand.

- The support of strategies to encourage research and development and the continual improvement of forensic science technology.
- Actively discourage behaviour that will bring the forensic science profession into disrepute.
- Discharge our responsibilities toward the public, our employers, our employees and peers in accordance with the ANZFSS 'Code of Ethics'.

South African Police Service

Code of Ethics

Ethical policing demands that we as employees of the South African Police Service act with integrity and respect for people's diversity and the law, thereby enhancing service excellence to the approval of the public.

As members of the South African Police Service we will perform our duties according to the following principles:

1. Integrity
   Application: Employees of the SAPS regard the truth as being of the utmost importance.
   Explanation: We, as the employees of the SAPS, continually strive to uphold the mission, values, ethical principles and ethical standards of the SAPS. We will behave in a manner, which is consistent with these values. We will act honestly and responsibly in all situations. We will always tell the truth, perform our duties with noble motives and set an example in the communities we serve.
2. Respect for diversity
   Application: Employees of the SAPS acknowledge the diversity of the people of our country and treat every person with equal respect.
   Explanation: In performing our duties, we will always show respect for the cultural and other diversities in the community. We will treat every person with equal respect and honour their rights as inhabitants of South Africa. We will not unlawfully discriminate against any person.
3. Obedience of the law
   Application: Employees of the SAPS respect and uphold the law at all times.
   Explanation: Our duties mainly involve enforcing the law, and in our application of the law we will always stay within the law and Constitution of our country. We will, at all costs, avoid any con-

duct which would make us violators of the law. We will protect the inhabitants of South Africa against unlawful actions.

4. Service excellence

Application: Employees of the SAPS work towards service excellence.

Explanation: We will, at all times, perform our duties to the best of our abilities. Our conduct will bear the mark of professionalism. Our conduct and appearance will be proof of our commitment to service excellence.

5. Public approval

Application: Employees of the SAPS always work with and for the approval of the community.

Explanation: We will serve the best interest of the community, seeking the approval of the broad community in everything we do.

Code of Conduct

I commit myself to creating a safe and secure environment for all people in South Africa by —

- participating in endeavours aimed at addressing the causes of crime;
- preventing all acts which may threaten the safety or security of any community; and
- investigating criminal conduct which endangers the safety or security of the community and bringing the perpetrators to justice.

In carrying out this commitment, I shall at all times —

- uphold the Constitution and the law;
- take into account the needs of the community;
- recognize the needs of the South African Police Service as my employer; and
- cooperate with all interested parties in the community and the government at every level.

In order to achieve a safe and secure environment for all the people of South Africa I undertake to —

- act with integrity in rendering an effective service of a high standard which is accessible to everybody, and continuously strive towards improving this service;
- utilize all available resources responsibly, efficiently and cost-effectively to optimize their use;
- develop my own skills and contribute towards the development of those of my colleagues to ensure equal opportunities for all;

- contribute to the reconstruction and development of, and reconciliation in our country;
- uphold and protect the fundamental rights of every person;
- act in a manner that is impartial, courteous, honest, respectful, transparent and accountable;
- exercise the powers conferred upon me in a responsible and controlled manner; and
- work towards preventing any form of corruption and to bring the perpetrators thereof to justice.

Bibliography

Agres, T. 2005. "When the Line Between Science and Business Blurs." *The Scientist*, February 28.

Ariely, D. 2008. *Predictably Irrational: The Hidden Forces That Shape Our Decisions*. New York: Harper Collins Publishers.

Armstrong, K. 2007. "Forensic Scientist Defends Work for State Patrol." *Seattle Times*, April 30.

Associated Press. 2006. "Most Unethical Federal Scientists Go Unpunished," September 12.

Associated Press. 2007a. "Expert's Ruse Raises Legal Questions." *USA Today*, March 9. Available at: http://www.usatoday.com/news/nation/2007-03-09-ballistics-expert_N.htm

Associated Press. 2007b. "N.C. Bar Files Ethics Charges against Duke Lacrosse Prosecutor," December 28.

Associated Press. 2008. *LAPD: False Arrests over Fingerprint Errors*, October 17.

Barnett, P. 2001. *Ethics in Forensic Science*. Boca Raton, FL: CRC Press.

Barrett, P. 2002. Standards for the Practice of Criminalistics. *Journal of Forensic Science*. [A Volume in the Protocols in Forensic Science Series], 47 (5).

Bauer, H.H. 1994. *Scientific Literacy and the Myth of the Scientific Method*. Champaign: University of Illinois Press.

Bird, F. 1996. *The Muted Conscience: Moral Silence and the Practice of Ethics in Business*. Westport, CT: Quorum.

Bird, S. 2001. "Scientific Uncertainty: Research versus Forensic Perspectives." *Journal of Forensic Science*, 46 (4): 978–981.

Black, H.C. 1990. *Black's Law Dictionary* (6th Edition). St. Paul, MN: West Publishing Company.

Bone, J. 2007. "CSI: Underpants Sees Scientist Dismissed over Test That Trapped Cheating Husband." *Times Online*, August 22.

Bovee, W. 1991. "The End Can Justify the Means—But Rarely." *Journal of Mass Media Ethics*, 6 (3): 135–145.

Bowen, R. 2006. *Ethics in Forensic Science* (Online Course). Morgantown: West Virginia University Forensic Science Initiative.

Braswell, M., B.R. McCarthy, and B.J. McCarthy. 2005. *Justice, Crime and Ethics* (5th Edition). Cincinnati: LexisNexis.

Braswell, M., B.R. McCarthy, and B.J. McCarthy. 2008. *Justice, Crime and Ethics* (6th Edition). Newark, NJ: LexisNexis.

Bronowski, J. 1956. *Science and Human Values*. Gloucester, MA: Peter Smith Publishers, Inc.

Ciulla, J. 2000. *The Working Life: The Promise and Betrayal of Modern Work*. New York: Times Books.

Ciulla, J. 2004. *Ethics, the Heart of Leadership*. Westport, CT: Praeger Publishers.

Clickondetroit.com. 2008. "Crime Lab Error Leads to New Murder Trial." September 25. Available at: http://www.clickondetroit.com/news/17556181/detail.html

Cohen, H. and M. Feldberg. 1991. Power and Restraint: The Moral Dimension of Police Work. New York: Praeger Press.

Condlin, R. 2003. "What's Love Got to Do with It? It's Not Like They're Your Friends for Christ's Sake: The Complicated Relationship between Lawyer and Client." *University of Nebraska Law Review,* 82: 211–311.

Couzin, J. 2006. "Fake Data, but Could the Idea Still Be Right?" *Science,* 313: 154 (July 14).

Couzin, J. 2006. "Truth and Consequences." *Science,* 313: 1222–1226 (September 1).

Couzin, J. and K. Unger. 2006. "Cleaning Up the Paper Trail." *Science,* 312: 38–43 (April 7).

Dahlberg, J. and C. Mahler. 2006. "The Poehlman Case: Running Away from the Truth." *Science and Engineering Ethics,* 12 (1): 157–173.

Daubert v. Merrell Dow Pharmaceuticals, Inc., 509 U.S. 579 (1993).

Daubert v. Merrell Dow Pharmaceuticals, Inc., 951 F. 2d 1128 (9th Cir. 1991).

Daubert v. Merrell Dow Pharmaceuticals, Inc., 727 F. Supp. 570, 574 (S.D.Cal, 1989).

Djerassi, C. 1991. *Cantor's Dilemma.* New York: Penguin Books.

Edel, A. 1955. *Ethical Judgment: The Use of Science in Ethics.* New York: Free Press.

Encarta World English Dictionary. "democracy." http://encarta.msn.com/dictionary-/democracy.html

Fanelli, D. 2009. How many scientists fabricate and falsify research? A systematic review and meta-analysis of survey data. *PLoS ONE* 4(5): e5738.cloi 10.1371/journal.pone.0005738.

Fed. R. Evid. 1988, 702.

Ferrazzi, K. Inc.com column. Article titled "Nepotism pays." No date available.

Fisher, B. 2000. *Techniques of Crime Scene Investigation* (6th Edition). Boca Raton, FL: CRC Press.

Fleckstein, M., M. Martone, and H. Pitluck. 2001. "Law, Ethical Codes, and the Report of the CSSP Survey on Ethical Policies." *Journal of Forensic Science,* 46 (4): 982–985.

Frankel, M. 1989. "Ethics and the Forensic Sciences: Professional Autonomy in the Criminal Justice System." *Journal of Forensic Sciences,* 34 (3): 763–771 (May).

Frye v. United States, 54 App. D.C. 46, 47, 293 F. 1013, 1014 (1923).

Garrison, D. 2004. "Precision without Accuracy in the Cruel World of Crime Scene Work." *Midwestern Association of Forensic Sciences Newsletter,* April.

Garrison, D. 1992. "Bad Science." *Midwestern Association of Forensic Sciences Newsletter,* July.

Gershman, B. 2003. "The Use and Misuse of Forensic Evidence." *Oklahoma City University Law Review,* 28: 17–41.

Goff, L. 2000. *A Fly for the Prosecution: How Insect Evidence Helps Solve Crimes.* Cambridge, MA: Harvard University Press.

Goodstein, D. 2002. "Scientific Misconduct." *Academe Online,* 88 (1), January–February. Available at: http://www.aaup.org/AAUP/pubsres/academe/2002/JF/

Grant, B. 2009. "Biotech's Baddies." *The Scientist,* April, 46–54.

Hardwig, J. 1991. "The Role of Trust in Knowledge." *Journal of Philosophy* 88: 693–708.

Harvard Business School Press and J.L. Badaracco. 2003. *Harvard Business Review on Corporate Ethics.* Boston: Harvard Business School Publishing Corporation.

Hollien, H. 1990. "The Expert Witness: Ethics and Responsibilities." *Journal of Forensic Sciences,* 35 (6): 1414–1423 (November).

Houck, M. and J. Siegel. 2006. *Fundamentals of Forensic Science.* Burlington, MA: Elsevier Academic Press.

Huicochea, A. 2008. "Drugs Gone from Crime Lab; Supervisor Resigns." *Arizona Daily Star,* April 26.

Johannesen, R., K. Valde, and K. Whedbee. 2008. *Ethics in Human Communication* (6th Edition). Long Grove, IL: Waveland Press, Inc.

Johnson, T. 2008. "State Crime Lab Chief Resigns after Problems Raised on DUI Evidence." *Seattle Post-Intelligencer,* February 14.

Josephson Institute for the Advancement of Ethics. 1988. "Ethics: Easier Said than Done," 1 (1): 153.

Kant, I. 1964. *Groundwork of the Metaphysics of Morals* (trans. H.J. Paton). New York: Harper & Row.

Kates, J. and H. Guttenplan. 1983. "Ethical Considerations in Forensic Science Services." *Journal of Forensic Sciences,* 28 (4): 972–976 (October).

Kovac, J. 2004. *The Ethical Chemist: Professionalism and Ethics in Science.* Upper Saddle River, NJ: Pearson Prentice Hall.

Leufkens, H. 1994. "Premature or Inappropriate Publication of Research Findings." *American Journal of Pharmaceutical Education,* 58: 95–97 (Spring).

Lilly, S. 2007. "Blood on the Courthouse Floor; Six U.S. Attorneys Fired. Why?" *Center for American Progress,* January 19. Available at: http://www.american-progress.org/issues/2007/01/court.html

Lucas, D. 1989. "The Ethical Responsibilities of the Forensic Scientist: Exploring the Limits," *Journal of Forensic Sciences,* 34 (3): 719–729 (May).

Lucas, D. 2007. "Forensic Science and Ethics—An Essential Association," presented at NERFI, MSP DNA Course, July 12.

Macrina, F. 2000. *Scientific Integrity.* Washington, DC: ASM Press.

Martin, M. 2007. *Creativity: Ethics and Excellence in Science.* Lanham, MD: Lexington Books.

Martyn, S. 2003. "In Defense of Client–Lawyer Confidentiality." *University of Nebraska Law Review,* 81: 1320–1350.

Mayo, D. and R. Hollander. 1991. *Acceptable Evidence.* New York: Oxford University Press.

McDonnell Social Norms Group. 2006. "Battling Bad Behavior." *Scientist,* February, 53–57.

McGee, G. 2006. "Lies, Damn Lies…and Scientific Misconduct." *The Scientist,* February, p. 24.

Memory J. and C. Rose. 2002. "The Attorney as Moral Agent: A Critique of Cohen." *Criminal Justice Ethics,* 21 (1): 28–39.

Model Rules of Professional Conduct. 2002. American Bar Association.

Moon, C. and C. Bonny. 2001. *Business Ethics.* London: Economist Newspaper Ltd.

Moran, D. and S. Gross. 2008. "Put Scientists, Not Cops, in Crime Labs," November 8. Available at: http://truthinjusticefiles.blogspot.com/2008/11/guest-shot-put-scientists-not-cops-in.html

Moran, G. 2006. "Criminalist Who Testified on DUIs Falsified Résumés." *San Diego Union-Tribune,* March 22. Available at: http://www.signonsandiego.com/uniontrib/20060322/news_7m22duiguy.html

Moxley, S. 2008. "CSI Games: If DNA Evidence Doesn't Fit in Orange County, Alter It?" *OC Weekly,* March 13.

National Research Council. 2009. *Strengthening Forensic Science in the United States: A Path Forward.* Washington, DC: National Academies Press. Available for free at: http://www.nap.edu/catalog.php?record_id=12589#toc

Nordby, J. 2002. "Review of: *Ethics in Forensic Science: Professional Standards for the Practice of Criminalistics [A Volume in the Protocols in Forensic Science Series].*" *Journal of Forensic Sciences,* 47 (5) (September).

North, S. 2001. "Patrol Chemist Faces Misdemeanor Counts." *Washington Herald,* January 26.

Oxford University Press. 2000. "Egoism." Oxford English Dictionary Online, Oxford University Press. April 4, p. 29. Available with subscription at: http://dictionary.oed.com/cgi/entry/00181778

Peterson, J. 1988. "Teaching Ethics in a Forensic Science Curriculum." *Journal of Forensic Sciences,* 33 (4): 1081–1085 (July).

Peterson, J. and J. Murdock. 1989. "Forensic Science Ethics: Developing an Integrated System of Support and Enforcement." *Journal of Forensic Sciences,* 34 (3): 749–762 (May).

Pollock, J. 2004. *Ethics in Crime and Justice: Dilemmas and Decisions.* Belmont, CA: Wadsworth.

Rawls, J. 1971. *A Theory of Justice.* Cambridge: Harvard University Press. p. 26.

Resnik, D.B. 1998. *The Ethics of Science.* New York: Routledge.

Rogers, T. 2004. "Crime Scene Ethics: Souvenirs, Teaching Material, and Artifacts." *Journal of Forensic Science,* 49 (2): 307–311 (March).

Rokeach, M. 1973. *The Nature of Human Values.* New York: Free Press.

Rossner, M. 2006. "How to Guard against Image Fraud." *The Scientist,* March.

Sagan, C. 1992. *The Demon-Haunted World: Science as a Candle in the Dark.* New York: Ballantine Books.

Saks, M. 1989. "Prevalence and Impact of Ethical Problems in Forensic Science." *Journal of Forensic Science,* 34 (3): 772–793 (May).

Saviers, K. 2002. "Ethics in Forensic Science: A Review of the Literature on Expert Testimony." *Journal of Forensic Identification,* 52 (4): 449–462.

Schroeder, O. 1984. "Ethical and Moral Dilemmas Confronting Forensic Scientists." *Journal of Forensic Science,* 29 (4): 966–986 (October).

Shellenbarger, S. 2005. "How and Why We Lie at the Office: From Pilfered Pens to Padded Accounts." *Wall Street Journal,* March 25.

Shermer, M. 2006. "Fake, Mistake, Replicate." *Scientific American,* September.

Shiffman, M. 2000. *Ethics in Forensic Science and Medicine.* Springfield, IL: Charles C. Thomas Publisher, Ltd.

Smrz, M. 2002. "Ethics in Forensic Science: Professional Standards for the Practice of Criminalistics—Book Review." *Forensic Science Communications,* 4 (3) (July).

Souryal, S. 1998. *Ethics in Criminal Justice: In the Search of Truth* (2nd Edition). Cincinnati, OH: Anderson Publishing Co.

Souryal, S. 2003. *Ethics in Criminal Justice: In Search of the Truth* (3rd Edition). Albany, NY: Matthew Bender & Company, Inc., a member of the LexisNexis Group.

Thomas, M. 1999. *Ethics in Forensic Science and Medicine: Guidelines for the Forensic Expert and the Attorney.* Springfield, IL: Charles Thomas Publisher Ltd.

Weinstock, R. 1986. "Ethical Concerns Expressed by Forensic Psychiatrists." *Journal of Forensic Sciences,* 31 (2): 596–602 (April).

Weinstock, R. 1988. "Controversial Ethical Issues in Forensic Psychiatry: A Survey." *Journal of Forensic Sciences,* 33 (1): 176–186 (January).

Welner, M. 2002. "Hired Gun." *Forensic Echo,* 2 (1) (March 11).

Welner, M. 2002. "The Dog Ate My Integrity." *Forensic Echo,* 3 (2) (March 11).

Weston, A. 2001. *A 21st Century Ethical Toolbox.* New York: Oxford University Press.

Wilbanks, W. 1987. *The Myth of a Racist Criminal Justice System.* Monterey, CA: Brooks/Cole Publishing.

Wilson, D. 2007. "Prosecutor in Duke Case Disbarred by Ethics Panel." *New York Times,* June 17.

Wilson, D. and D. Barstow. 2007. "All Charged Dropped in Duke Case." *New York Times,* April 12.

Wilson, D. 2006. "Crime Lab Investigation." *Guardian,* September 14.

Wishman, S. 1981. *Confessions of a Criminal Lawyer.* New York: Penguin Books.

Zajac, A. 2007. "Pointing the Way for Prosecutors: Under Fire, not in Retreat Gonzales' Plan for Attorney Reviews Would Further Politicize Process." *Chicago Tribune,* June 17. Available at: http://archives.chicagotribune.com/2007/jun17/news/chi-gonzales_thinkjun17.

Index